Manal Tamimi, Pa
Paul Morris, Peter Lanti

AHED TAMIMI
A GIRL WHO FOUGHT BACK

To Nariman and Bassem Tamimi

VAKTEL BOOKS/VAKTEL FÖRLAG

Vaktel Books/Vaktel förlag
Box 3027
S-630 03 Eskilstuna
Sweden
www.vaktelforlag.se
admin@vaktelforlag.se

Copyright © 2018 The authors
Cover design: Dennis Rudd *dennis@kavitagraphics.co.uk*
Insert layout: Henny Östlund *henny.ostlund@gmail.com*
Cover photo: Haim Schwarczenberg
Printing: Printon Publishing House, Estonia
ISBN 978-91-88441-26-3

Index

Birthday… and Trial

A letter from Bassem Tamimi to his daughter Ahed on the occasion of her 17th birthday, 31 January 2018.

To my daughter, Ahed,
To be able to write you in a moment like this, I had to lay down in your bed. Then, when I rested my head on your little pillow, you recharged my soul. It was charged to the brim with gratitude for the memory of your generosity. How can my spirit not be lifted when you were the one who brought the world to a storm, like a hurricane?

My courageous, beautiful, shy, and bold little girl – victory is befitting of you as much as joy suits you. My daughter, I am so sorry I could not protect you from the ugliness of the Occupation. I am sorry I left the oranges of Yafa sad and unpeeled, yearning for your touch. You are now surrounded by bars of iron, in a place where time is stale, and freedom and love are non-existent. Yet, it is in that cell that my hope of a better future and the certainty we will achieve it is now placed. You, my ray of hope, are locked in a prison, which is built on the ruins of Imm Khaled, near the shore of our sea. The same Imm Khaled that was ethnically cleansed by the army you slapped.

Ahed, your cell, halfway to Haifa, on the route to which we will one day return. There, I imagine myself with you, the sound of my voice resonating from behind the walls – Ahed… Ahed… Ahed… My daughter, the strings of my soul – may each year see you shine brighter with the truth you hold inside. May each year see you stronger, more joyful, and as solid as the rocks that hold back the rage of oceans.

Happy birthday

When parents celebrate their children's birthdays, we try to make them special and unforgettable – worthy of this wondrous occasion. As parents, these days bring a soft and graceful joy to our hearts.

Today is your birthday, but I woke up in the middle of the night, not with excitement, but -uncomfortable and short of breath. This birthday of yours, different than the ones before it. Yes, it is the day you were born in, but you are forcefully kept farther away than I can bare. Still, you are closer to my heart than you could ever imagine.

Today, my daughter, you are a year wiser – a year filled with an even deeper love for your homeland. Today you enter a year that will be harder than those that preceded it. I dread the thought of your prison nights and the knowledge of their chill.

Prison nights are not like those at home, with us. The commotion of birthday parties is a stark contrast to the loneliness of the prison cell they have you in. I am so sorry. All I want is to gently stroke your golden hair my little girl, as I've done since you were a baby; to tenderly embrace you, after you blow out the 17 candles on your birthday cake, like I have done since you turned one. But how can my longing for you break through those bars of steel that are now placed between us?

Do not worry Ahed, we will see joy again and celebrate as we always have. I hereby promise, your brothers and I will stand at the gates of prison and sing for you and your mother's freedom. We will demand the freedom of all those imprisoned unjustly; we will demand freedom for all free spirits. And you and your mother will sing with us, and pound on the prison walls with your mighty power.

Tonight we will celebrate your birthday by showing the world that no matter what happens, we celebrate life. We teach life. We love life and will not let this love be squashed. Never.

But until this evening comes when we celebrate together as a family, I wish you to stay strong and resilient. I know the soldiers may come at midnight, shackle you, and drag you through another interrogation session. If you can dress warmly, put on an extra shirt, because they will do their best to take away the warmth. Every room they will put you in, every military vehicle, will be freezing cold, on purpose. But I know I need not worry. I know how warm your soul is. You shouldn't be, you really shouldn't be, my little girl, but I know that you can take whatever darkness and coldness they try and torture you with.

Whatever decision it will make, the Israeli military court you will be tried in will not give you justice. These courts were not built to bring justice, these judges do not desire justice. They were built in a realm outside of humanity. 99% of those who stand before them are found guilty. But these are all just the symptoms of the illness – even if you are acquitted, these courts cannot ever be a tool of justice, since they are just another cog in the machine of military Occupation. Colonialism and the basic values of mankind will never cross paths. The Occupation can never intersect with freedom, justice, and dignity.

Humanity is beautiful. It paints life with a brush of grace and endows it with beauty. The Occupation is ugly, and it is made to disfigure the face of humanity. My daughter, free people do not get lost in their own narcissism, for none of us alone are anything if we do not connect to a deeper purpose and do not dedicate ourselves to positive action. It is through our deep connection, purpose, and action that we move from the solitary conditions of our birth to the real meaning and preciousness that the world has to offer. It is this awareness that allows humanity and collective consciousness. You, my little girl, have tapped into that consciousness of all humanity.

They take you to trial because they want to kill that sense of humanity that is in you; they want to destroy your sense of collective struggle for a better world. It is too dangerous for them to handle. Believe it or not, they are even trying to take away your youth saying that, as you turn 17, you are a child no more. And I ask, does your childhood take a different path than you yourself on the day of 17, or does your childhood have a little more time to play in the orchards of youth and enjoy the last of your school days in peace?

Israel's experts in immoral law may freely deliberate the unlawfulness of the slap served to their fully armed soldier by a girl which shattered their military manliness and put their fragile institutions at risk of collapse. Let them. Care not about their immoral military laws, for these laws are outside of the confines of humanity.

My little angel… Do not bother yourself with the words of those who trade in politics and religion like merchants in the market. Religious men, pious in their own eyes, want to discuss your hair in order to take attention away from your struggle and its legitimacy. The indoctrinated, unadulterated in their own eyes, do not recognize the humanity and truth in anyone who does not blindly plead loyalty to their dogma.

Then there are those who are always absent; the ones who refuse to take a stance for that which is right, who shiver at the idea of standing up in the face of oppression. They refuse to confront brutality; and those who struggle *for* freedom, like you, tear off their masks to show them for what they are.

Don't worry about those who criticize you now, my little girl. Your bravery has turned you into a lightning rod and those who fear their own hypocrisy being revealed want to hide by hurting you. All their criticism of you is made up so that they can continue to hide behind their fears. They know, it is your courage that has reminded everyone – the emperor has no clothes.

Here you stand before the world – like days past and days to come – full of truth because you were raised to be honest with yourself and others, and you have learned from our land and history that true freedom comes from having agency. It comes from being willing to challenge fear time and time again. To refuse to give up your dignity.

Now your tiny slap has shaken their mighty, blood-thirsty military to the core and shattered their symbolic deterrence. Your own personal truth is our truth, the truth of our historical and human struggle to stay on this land. It challenges the false narratives they have, about us and of themselves.

Your truth now carries with it a whole generation that has refused to surrender to oppression, a generation that will continue to fight for its freedom. Your truth shines through because you stood up for your community and your homeland and those you love. You refused to belong to anything but yourself and Palestine.

Your truth is purer than ever, because, in our day and age, in Palestine, those who are pure can be found in two places, either as political prisoners on the edge of freedom, or as martyrs who have been taken from us, and are now watching us in heaven. Your truth is now a beacon of hope for people around the world who have chosen to resist oppression instead of succumbing to it.

Do not worry, my little daughter – your freedom, as is the end of the Occupation is near. And those who stood against our freedom – the hypocrites and extremists and cowards – will be left with nothing but disappointment when history is written.

When I return home tonight, I will go to your room with your brothers and we will light a candle for you, and feel your presence with us, chanting that you are our "Ahed", our promise for a better world; like an Olive Tree grounded in the earth.

Your mother is waiting for you back in prison. If you get to see her, please hug her for me, and celebrate your birthday together with us in your hearts. And if you are kept alone until dawn in their metal boxes, just take a seat on the saddle of hope, rise up on the horse of courage you have imagined since you were a little girl, do not pay attention to those who want to deceive and hurt you, just look at the sun rise from the small hatch and shine your smile back at it, for it is your smile that will bring us towards a brighter future.

I miss you Ahed, but I say happy birthday. May every year that comes make you stronger. May you always be full of love and bursting with truth.

Your loving father

Publisher's Introduction

That a 16-year-old Palestinian schoolgirl was suddenly and brutally sent to a military prison inside Israel was a profound shock to me, and millions of people around the world. Later, I watched a short video clip – filmed by the Israeli military – showing how a group of large, strong Israeli soldiers in full battle gear, holding that girl, Ahed Tamimi, in a firm grip, force her to rush from the front door of her home and to an Israeli military vehicle, into which she is shoved. Thirty years ago, we saw policemen of the Apartheid regime in South Africa arrest ANC militants in that way. But those militants were big, strong men, and most often they had resisted the arrest violently – hence provoking such a rough handling.

But this was a young girl who was supposed to go to school the next morning, which was a Wednesday. On her desk in her bedroom lay a paper, her completed homework from school. Instead of handing in her work to her teacher after breakfast, and other civilised routines – she is forced out of her bed in the middle of the night. Before she really knew what had happened, a steel door slammed in front of her, locking her into a cell in a grim, military prison.

When I learned about this on the news here in Sweden, I was absolutely stunned. As a father of two daughters, I could imagine the horror she must have felt, woken up by foreign soldiers breaking into her home in the middle of the night – and they were after *her*. I also felt for her father. I did the only thing I could do; I wrote a message to him, Bassem Tamimi, to his Facebook page to express sympathy and offer solidarity in the campaign to free Ahed.

I knew that she had slapped an Israeli soldier, but that could not justify her arrest. I had seen the video, made by Ahed's mother four days previously, on 15 December 2017. It showed two armed Israeli soldiers entering what I now know to be the Tamimi family's garden, and Ahed and Nour being very upset and telling them to leave. Of course they were upset. Only minutes before, an Israeli soldier had shot Ahed's

15-year-old cousin Mohammad Tamimi straight in the face, at close range with a rubber-coated steel bullet, leading him to be placed in an induced coma, before life-saving surgery. And now the same soldiers entered the Tamimi family's garden, without any obvious reason.

The video clip shows how a heated argument starts between the two soldiers and the two little girls, who barely reach to the shoulders of the two uniformed men. The Israeli soldiers refuse to leave. One of the soldiers starts waving his hand at Ahed and strikes her in order to push her back. Ahed reacts in the wink of an eye and slaps back, hitting the soldier. What would the soldiers have done, had Ahed's mother not been filming the scene?

In any case, they do show restraint. While the other soldier continues the discussion with the two girls, the one who has received the slapping turns his back to the camera and turns passive. The video clip of Ahed girl hitting back and slapping a representative of the Israeli Army, without being immediately punished for that, created an uproar of rage in the Israeli community. Some were furious at the soldiers for not having replied with violence, some even said that the girl should have been shot. Powerful voices were calling for retaliation.

Along with many others, I was aware of the Israeli occupation policy and the repeated criticism that had been levelled against Israel for repeated violations of human rights. The state of Israel has lost probably most of its friends in the world because of this. But I imagined that the oppression had not reached a level where school-girls were thrown into jail, and for such a minor offence. The following days and weeks would teach me that I had been naive.

Christmas passed and New Year came. Slowly, it stood clear to the world that the State of Israel was intent on setting an example with this girl. She was not going to be released as quickly as I and many others had imagined. And more so, when her mother went to visit her in prison, she too was arrested.

I had seen Ahed on YouTube several times in the past years. Labelled as "the brave little girl", her desperate and brave challenging of Israeli soldiers had gone viral on a few occasions. The first time was five years ago, when a clip showed an eleven-year-old Ahed crying desperately, hugging her mother who was in the process of being shoved into a military vehicle by half-a-dozen Israeli soldiers. It was heart-wrenching, something that you don't forget. And now, when she was sixteen, she was in prison.

I felt that I had to do something. I managed to get her father's phone number and called him. We spoke for a couple of minutes. There was a special bond there, between two fathers. I heard myself ask Bassem if he would accept that I, as a publisher, published a book about Ahed. The world has to learn to know her, and if a book about her can help her in this situation, it is the least I can do, being a publisher. On the other side of the line, Bassem told me that he accepted.

Two days later, my friend Paul Morris, a university lecturer in Sweden, with a thorough knowledge about the situation in Palestine, had taken on the project with compassion and great enthusiasm. Paul in turn got his colleague, Paul Heron, a well-known UK lawyer, strongly engaged in human rights issues, aboard. Peter Lahti, a journalist with the same social pathos, joined and these three created a strong and very dedicated team.

Very soon, Paul and Paul were in almost daily contact with various members of the the Tamimi family. They began to plan for a visit to the Tamimi's village on the West Bank, Nabi Saleh. That called for a visit to the Embassy of Palestine, in Stockholm, where we all received a friendly reception and were supplied with some very good leads for the upcoming visit to the West Bank.

The visit by Paul and Paul in the West Bank was decisive, of course. While Peter was at home, working on the manuscript, the Pauls, with Bassem's support introductions met with many people crucial to the struggle in Nabi Saleh, filmed, made interviews and listened. They told me how the image of Ahed developed in their minds, hour by hour.

A crucial contact was made with Ahed's aunt, Manal Tamimi. The long conversations with Manal made it clear that we had to bring Manal along the board of authors, and it was most fortunate that she willingly agreed to join along. Both Pauls had realised that Manal, in telling them her story and thoughts, was obviously an author, and had a crucial chapter to add on the women's struggle to liberate Palestine.

When Paul and Paul came back home, they could tell me a story of a family who believed strongly in peaceful means in order to get back a normal, decent life; they told me of a young girl who wanted nothing but to be able to live like any other girl of her age, to study at school, to hang around with her friends, to go swimming in the nearby ocean, to play football – a girl who was prevented from all of that because of a brutal occupation; a girl whose father and mother are over and over again taken away from her to be sent into prison, although they have never committed any violent action in their whole life, never committed a single crime; a girl whose aunt and uncle have been killed by soldiers while they themselves were unarmed and posed no threat whatsoever; a girl who is slandered by right-wing Israelis and has even received death threats. A girl who just wanted to be a girl, but who has had to fight back.

For that reason, it is necessary to tell the world her story.

The intention of this book, which will be translated into several languages, is to tell Ahed Tamimi's story and the context in which she lives, a context that is very hard to apprehend for anyone not experiencing it. Vaktel Books is an ordinary commercial publishing house with a wide range of books, but this book is a solidarity project. Half the profits from this book are donated to the Palestine Legal Defence Fund. When Ahed was taken prisoner she joined hundreds of other child political prisoners held in the military jails of Israel. The legal fight costs money, and this book will hopefully raise both funds for that fight and help raise awareness, and help build a campaign to win their release, and, indeed, end the military occupation of Palestine. The Palestine Legal Defence Fund can be reached via www.ahedtamimibook.com.

Eskilstuna, Sweden, 13 March 2018
Christer Bergström, publisher at Vaktel Books

Acknowledgments

The authors owe a great debt of gratitude to the following persons, who have rendered the work on this book an invaluable assistance:

Bassem Tamimi.

Hala Fariz, Ambassador of Palestine, Sweden.

Cindy Inglessis, Assistant to the Palestinian Ambassador in Sweden.

Janna Jihad, the youngest journalist in the world (for the interviews).

Nour Tamimi (for the interview).

Marah Tamimi (for the interview).

Nawal Tamimi (for the interview).

Bilal Tamimi, Nariman Tamimi, Heidi Levine, Ahmad Gharabli and Haim Schwarzenberg for the use of their fantastic images.

Hamdi Bawaqneh, Diana Mosa, Mohamed Mosa and Mariam Massoud for translation help.

Peter Hill, for the videos.

Keely Kingswood and Louise Jones for the great transcription services, sometimes without the highest quality recordings.

Jeffrey Lark, Suzy Morris and Sarah Hall Preston for helpful contributions and reflections.

Lennart Wennergrund for the website.

DCI who kindly let us use some graphics.

Protest Stencil for letting us use their images.

The brave people of Nabi Saleh.

Should anyone have been omitted above, it is by pure mistake, for which the authors and the publishers ask for apology; please regard this as our implied gratitude.

CHAPTER 1

Ahed Tamimi

Some days before Christmas last year (2017) I saw the video on You-Tube. The video had gone viral. I don't recall seeing any names for the protagonists at first – strangers from the anonymous world of the internet. It's a fight, nothing unusual in that, in terms of what does the viral rounds on YouTube – but it's a strange and uneven fight. There's a girl, a fairly ordinary teenage girl, in a typical denim jacket, nothing unusual there either. But the opponent… now that's strange, a fully kitted out, uniformed and armed soldier. The scene goes viral because the unarmed teenage *girl next-door* is standing up to a soldier. A closer look will tell you who it is, it's Ahed Tamimi, 16 years old. A Palestinian girl, in the front drive of her own home, standing up to a representative of a vicious military occupation, an Israeli soldier abroad, in the village of Nabi Saleh in the West Bank.

Like with so many YouTube clips or pictures on the internet it is easy for a scene to be taken out of context, and I remember watching this video, half sleepily, in my Facebook feed. I confess that I didn't know what was going on, only half concentrating, in that endless stream of information and images we get now online. I admit too that I at first saw the girl's seeming aggression and the soldier's seeming restraint. But that is to misread the picture. What is going on in the picture is actually remarkable. Whilst the scene is a front drive of a house, like any other, there are, however, intruding soldiers, from an occupying force. Soldiers from another country have entered the garden of a private house. The young women in the video clip, there are two of them after the start, Ahed Tamimi (16 years old at the time of the incident), and Nour Tamimi (20 years old) are telling the soldiers to go away.

"Leave!" is the plea, and, of course, they want them out of their drive quickly, and, eventually, out of their country too.

And, reader, I think you need to think how you would hope to act, were soldiers from an occupying land in your front garden. Would you cower behind your window? Duck down behind your settee? Or could you be as brave as Ahed and Nour, and go out and confront them?

If you did, would you be calm and restrained, for the eyes of the world? Here I think some empathy is called for. Prior to the above incident, the scene that went viral, Ahed and Nour's cousin, their young cousin, Mohammad Tamimi, just 15 years of age, has just been shot at close range in the head by the Israeli Defence Force (IDF). His injuries are so severe he will have to be put into an induced coma for the operation. His life will possibly never be the same again. The rubber-coated steel bullet had broken his jaw on entry through his face, into his skull. On this day, with Mohamed's life on a thread, some IDF soldiers want to take cover in Ahed's drive so as to be better placed to shoot at some more youths down the road. Ahed and Nour have other ideas, and they go out to tell the soldiers that there will be no safe haven for them here.

They will not be able to hide behind this wall and take shots.

This is the resistance to the Occupation by the Tamimi family. The Tamimi family is armed too, not with guns, but with the powerful weapon of the camera, and access to the internet. The incident is being filmed and, to a degree the soldiers, mindful of the cameras, are relatively restrained. Though one of them does forcefully attempt to brush Ahed aside, the soldiers receive a contemptuous volley of words and blows from the girls to persuade them to leave. And they do leave, for the time being.

But, the soldiers will be back, in greater numbers and in the dark, away from the light that feeds the cameras, and the wakeful eyes of many witnesses. As the Washington Post newspaper's motto states – *Democracy Dies in Darkness*; instead *fear* thrives, and the occupying soldiers feed on fear.

The IDF comes back, a few nights after the viral video incident. They come in the middle of the night, at around 3am. They wake the family and take Ahed away, to an Israeli military jail. As I write, many weeks have passed, months even, since that night raid and Ahed is still in an Israeli military jail. That Ahed is held outside of her homeland means she is being held illegally, under the rules of the Geneva Convention, which dictate that a prisoner cannot simply be taken to another country, to the country of the aggressor, the occupier.

In total, Ahed would face a long series of charges for violence and incitement, covering a period going back twenty months. Ahed's mother, Nariman, had gone down to the police station on the morning following Ahed's arrest to protest but was not allowed to return home. She too was charged, and imprisoned, until a trial that would be put back and put back. Nour was arrested the night after Ahed's arrest and she would be charged too.

At Ahed's appearance at the Ofer military court, Jerusalem, on 1 January 2018, she smiled defiantly, giving strength to her supporters and family, but also giving an image seized upon by the massed media photographers. The Palestinian movement, in Ahed, had a young, living, and vibrant symbol of their struggle. Her long, fair coloured hair was let down and flowed, perhaps mane-like, so that some commentators would compare her to a courageous lion. This powerful image would be spread, of a fiery young political prisoner – a girl that fought back.

*

Some weeks later I'm sitting in a café in the Palestinian town of Ramallah and I'm interviewing Ahed's father, Bassem. In order to interview him, and other members of Ahed's family and friends, for this book I had travelled, with a lawyer and friend, Paul Heron. I was determined, with this book, to help ensure that the imprisonment of Ahed would not lead to her being silenced, that her arrest and imprisonment would not be in vain. I hoped that her case and trial could allow the Occupation to be exposed, and that *it*, not Ahed would be put on trial before the eyes of the world.

I had seen Bassem on YouTube and seen pictures of him online. I had imagined him bigger, tougher even. I imagined him brutalised to some extent by his nine stints in prison. But his entrance into the Ramallah café suggested I was wrong. He is a graceful man, smaller than I had imagined, and is dressed smartly in a shirt and a coat, like a long suit jacket. He walks into the café and one or two men recognise him, and rise to greet him warmly and respectfully. In our introductions I feel he is dignified, with years of protest under his belt, and a steely determination. But his eyes become a little glassy when he talks of the soldiers taking away his only daughter, in the middle of a December night.

Bassem tells us about the last hours of Ahed being in her family home. His description of the night of his teenage daughter's arrest, takes us into the dark world of night raids, army boots in children's bedrooms, of the brutality of military occupation:

> "The media had started talking about what she is doing. I told her this night they will come to arrest you. She said I am ready and she goes to sleep normally.
>
> I look at her and she was sleeping, deeply sleeping and I went to sleep too.
>
> Then around 3 or 4 in the morning they came, [the IDF] banging the door, shouting, and shooting grenades of tear gas outside. This is not the first time. They have come to my home hundreds of times. But I saw that they are more aggressive, more angry, and then they told me to bring everyone to the living room. I bring them, her two brothers who were home, and Nariman comes too. They told me that they had come to arrest her (Ahed). I told them she needs to change from night clothes.

They refused to let her mother go with her to the bedroom. Instead, she went with two female soldiers. Within four minutes she was handcuffed and outside the home and they started searching the house. Everything upside down. They do not allow us to take any photos or recordings. They took all our electric devices, cameras, laptops, computer, sim cards, memories, everything, USBs, our phones, everything, they took everything. I noticed one of my sons didn't want to give them his phone and so six soldiers were on him trying to take it from him."

I asked Bassem how old the boys were:

"One is 11 (Salam) and the other is 14 (Abu Yazan) and the soldiers are upon them and want to take their phones. It takes them 40 minutes or so to search to house and we follow them. There is around 12 military vehicles, jeeps, cars, big armoured cars outside. I called to Ahed, now in one of the military armoured cars, and told her to keep strong. She replied: *Don't worry I know what I should do."*

Gaby Lasky, Ahed's lawyer, explained the pressure which had driven the IDF to arrest Ahed. Gaby, on the Electronic Intifada podcast (21 January 2018), said that the viral video of Ahed slapping the soldiers had fed two powerful narratives, different for both Palestinians and Israelis. For the Palestinians they had a freedom fighter in Ahed. The Israelis, on the other hand, felt for their soldiers, showing, in their eyes, restraint. Whipped up by the Israeli press and political leadership, this distorted into a fear that they were being humiliated. For them, Ahed would have to be taught a lesson.

A number of Israeli politicians and sections of the media had become hysterical about what they wanted to do to Ahed. For them it was too much she had stood up to the occupier. The Culture Minister

Miri Regev had felt "crushed" when watching the clip. The Israeli Education Minister, Naftali Bennett wanted Ahed and the other women in the video clip (by the end of the clip this included Nariman) to "spend the rest of their days in prison".

The response from Israeli journalist Ben Caspit was appalling. He wrote in an article in Hebrew: "In the case of the girls, we should exact a price at some other opportunity, in the dark, without witnesses and cameras."[1] What hideous deeds does he encourage them to act out away from the cameras? Beatings? Rape? Some sort of revenge far from watching eyes – that is for sure.

The army released a video clip of Ahed's arrest to the Israeli press to show that they had acted. They even took the unusual step of putting the IDF logo on the clip. The action itself, the arrest, and the need to go to the press, were a tribute to the power of Ahed. In recognition of the strength of Ahed as a potential symbol of revolt against the Occupation they put a blanket on the head of Ahed. They did not want to further her recognition in the world. Whilst they had to play to the home audience of Israel by showing that Ahed was being arrested they could not show to the whole world a picture of this fair haired girl – already known to many via the viral video – being bullied and captured in the night. In the language of marketing or PR – the *optics,* shorthand for how it would look in the media, would not be good, if Ahed could be easily recognised.

Back in the Ramallah Café Bassem described the morning after Ahed's arrest:

> "That morning I went to Ramallah to change my sim card so I could call a lawyer and to see what I shall do. Nariman, and her sister went to the police station. I was back around 9.30am, and the lawyer called me to say they had detained Nariman and had taken her for investigation."

Bassem explained that he was very worried about these investigations as he recalled one of his arrests in 1993 when he had been tortured, and even paralysed (temporarily) as a result. He gave a flavour of the treatment Ahed and Nariman could be getting in the military jails. Transport would be in a kind of metal box on the Borstar (armoured car), where if the weather was hot you would be left to be very hot, or if cold –very cold. Air conditioning would either be left off or turned to extremities – with discomfort the order of the day. Ahed and Nariman could be locked up with Israeli female criminals in close proximity – even settlers from the illegal settlements could be allowed to come in and taunt them.

Ahed had marathon investigation or interrogation sessions lasting from 1pm to 12.30am, with one officer from the police, and one from the army, alternating. She had not been allowed a change of clothes for the first days of her incarceration, and when she appeared in court she was handcuffed and shackled at the ankles. Initially, she had been taken to the Al-Moscobiyeh prison in Jerusalem – known in English as the Russian Compound. Bassem said it was the worst place to take children to. Gaby Lasky, Ahed's lawyer, complained that, although Ahed had the right to remain silent, she had been threatened with the mass arrest of members of her extended family, if she did not talk. Indeed, on 9 January 2018, 19 -year-old Mohammad Bilal Tamimi, (another of Ahed's cousins) was arrested. He, like Ahed, was also abducted from his Nabi Saleh home, in the middle of the night.

Indeed, the arrests from the village of Nabi Saleh, amongst the wider Tamimi family have continued, peaking at ten arrests on the night of 26 February 2018, where five minors were arrested. These included 15 -year-old Mohammad whose facial shooting and severe head injury had fuelled the December viral video incident. Mohammad's arrest was particularly vindictive as he was meant to be resting at home as he awaited skull restorative surgery.

For Ahed and the Tamimi family the New Year of 2018 has simply brought arrests, interrogations and court appearances where justice is known only for its absence. Nariman and Ahed were given court appearances only to be denied bail and Ahed was later moved to the Hasharon prison in, further into Israel. Nour was released on bail on 5 January, at a cost of 5,000 shekels ($1,450).

Ahed's prison guards, her interrogators, the military *so-called* judges would love to be able to deal with Ahed behind closed doors, away from the eyes of the world. That is why when Ahed was arrested in the middle of the night in December 2017 the IDF were quick to shroud her with a blanket. The same blanketing action would be carried out in the military court nearly two months later when the press were thrown out and a *closed court* declared, at another of Ahed's hearings (13 February 2018), where once again her trial was put back. But many people could understand that Ahed, and her family, were being treated harshly, and responded with angry protest.

As I write, nearly two million people have signed one petition alone to release her and other Palestinian children held in Israeli military prisons.[2] Indeed, such is the spread of the movement around freeing Ahed that there are, in fact, a whole batch of petitions. Many voices have been raised to demand her release. Michael Lynk, the United Nations special rapporteur on the situation of human rights in Palestine, stated that Ahed was being held pre-trial in an Israeli Military Prison against the convention on the rights of the child – itself ratified by Israel.[3] *Amnesty International* joined in, with an appeal to Israeli Prime Minister Netanyahu, to release Ahed, without any delay. In the *Amnesty* petition they call her the Rosa Parks of Palestine, a reference to the anti-racist civil rights campaigner from America who famously dared to sit in a "whites only" seat on an Alabama bus in the 1950s.

As Ahed's confinement continued into the first months of 2018, parliaments around the world responded to Ahed's unfair treatment. The Chilean Government requested the prompt release of Ahed.[4]

21 UK Labour Pary Members of Parliament sent a message of support to the Tamimi family. Even the UK Foreign Affairs minister, Alaister Burt, commented during questioning that the Israeli soldiers should not have been there to cause the incident which led to Ahed's arrest. In Ireland, Paul Murphy, (member of the Irish Dail – parliament) raised the case of Ahed.

The call to free Ahed, her mother, Nariman, and the hundreds of Palestinian child prisoners, was plastered over advertising boards on the bus stops of London by *@Protestencil,* in January 2018. As the protest spread around the globe over 700 young American Jewish people wrote letters to Ahed to mark her 17th birthday, these were delivered by dozens of Jewish activists to Bassem at the family home. One letter read:

> "Dear Ahed,
> My name is Shula and I am 17. We're [the] same age and we live in different worlds. Your courage inspires me to stand up for what I believe in. Your actions are not done in vain."[5]

On 12 February 2018, organisations representing over ten million women in India gave their support to the Free Ahed campaign; I heard in a subsequent phone call to Bassem how this news had cheered him. On the same day, dozens of prominent American figures including film stars, authors and campaigners such as Danny Glover, Rosario Dawson, Cornel West and Angela Davis signed a letter organised by Dream Defenders, demanding that Ahed be released.[6] Three days later, one of the signatories, comedian Sarah Silverman, who happens to be Jewish, tweeted "Jews have to stand up EVEN when – ESPECIALLY when – the wrongdoing is BY Jews/the Israeli government." A Twitter storm followed with Silverman getting lots of support internationally, but also a lot of condemnation, particularly from Israeli Jews.

A celebrity voice in Israel was raised *against* Ahed's arrest. Yehonaton Geffen, an Israeli poet, dared to write a poem where he compared

Ahed to Anne Frank, the Jewish girl who famously wrote her diaries about the occupation of The Netherlands by the Nazis during World War 2. However, the hail of protest against him was such that he dared not go out of the house for a week; he complained that he lost his appetite during the outcry. He felt he was under "house arrest", apologized, and retracted the poem.[7]

This air of witch-hunt in Israel is far from healthy. The Israeli state is actually in something of a crisis; the Prime Minister, Netanyahu, has been accused of corruption and faces charges associated with taking bribes of over $300,000. With his back to the wall, Netanyahu is desperate to shift attention and make a scapegoat of Ahed rather than attempt any kind of justice. It seems fair to say Netanyahu has a greater concern for business and trade than the fineries of humane and moral judgements; he was the first major foreign leader to formalise relations with the new Austrian government, which includes the far-right *Freedom Party* in the coalition.

Netanyahu, and the Israeli right wing, will try to paint Ahed as a monster, a terrorist. Accusers of Ahed will wheel in, as evidence, a mistranslated video of Ahed speaking on camera after the incident with the soldiers in her garden. The video's added subtitles suggest Ahed voices support for suicide bombers. She does no such thing, she calls for mass peaceful protest but declares that the blame for other forms of struggle will lie at the door of President Trump, for his declaration that Jerusalem is the Capital City of Israel – an insult to the Palestinian rights to the city. The right wing *Times of Israel* newspaper repeats the false claim that Ahed called for suicide bombings (they even add stabbings!). They give a flavour of the hysterics and false accusations which will be thrown at Ahed.[8]

A stereotype of Ahed will be painted by her accusers, but in defending her it is crucial that a mirror image stereotype is avoided. Ahed is rapidly becoming an icon for a freedom struggle. Indeed, Jim Fitzpatrick, the Irish artist, who drew the famous and iconic image of revolutionary fighter Che Guevara, has drawn a picture of Ahed as a brave wonder woman and has donated it without charge to the movement. It is marvelous that Ahed can be an iconic emblem for a positive movement to free Palestine. But it is vital that in response to the stereotyping of the right we avoid the trap of dichotomies, of over-simplification. Ahed is a human being and must be understood in terms of her humanity. Similarly, it needs to be understood that many of the Israeli occupying soldiers in Palestine are conscripts, forced to be in an army. Surely, the talents of Israeli youth could be harnessed elsewhere, in more productive capacities?

*

I was curious to learn more from Bassem about the earlier childhood of Ahed, so I asked him about what she was like as a young girl? In the Ramallah café, the toots of the cars in the busy street came through the window and I had to hold the phone close to his mouth to ensure I record his voice. He admitted he missed a lot of Ahed's childhood. He was in prison, for a total of three years, over nine occasions, without ever being charged – *administrative detention* – vague and colonial. Indeed, a relic from British rule. But his blue eyes moisten a little again, as he recounts how even in her baby-buggy the young Ahed was faced with checkpoints.

Bassem recalls how she maybe got a little tough, playing, play-fighting even, with her brothers – the only girl amongst three of them. But Bassem recalls generosity too, how she looked after the youngest brother, Salam, saving an ice cream for him and going without herself. Her other younger brother, Abu Yazan, she would later help free from the grip of an Israeli soldier in an earlier viral video (more of this later). This generosity can be seen too when Bassem tells of how Ahed had always wanted to be a footballer, but selflessly put these ambitions aside (later I meet her friend Marah who bears witness to this too). He recalls an occasion when Ahed came to visit him in prison and told him that her plans to be a footballer had been put on hold because she, instead, wanted to be a lawyer. The pride shines from him knowing that Ahed wanted to be a lawyer to help him fight for an end to political imprisonment, indeed to free Palestine.

Bassem feels Ahed *was* and *is* brave. But a price has been paid for this bravery and it creates a tension in Bassem. His pride for his daughter sits with an awareness of the weight of the loss – a childhood interrupted, a family torn apart.

Ahed was born on 31 January 2001, in the village of Nabi Saleh. The village was founded by Ahed's ancestors four hundred years ago. Nabi Saleh sits atop hills, some twenty kilometers north-west of Ramallah, in the West Bank. From the top of those hills, you can see the blue Mediterranean Sea, less than thirty kilometers to the west. But the children of Nabi Saleh can only look at the sea and dream about visiting it because they are barred from entering Israel.

Ahed was born in the midst of the so-called Second Intifada, the Palestinian wave of protest that was sparked off by a provocative walk held by Israel's Ariel Sharon, accompanied by over one thousand Israeli police officers, to the Temple Mount, the site of the al-Aqsa Mosque, in September 2000.[9]

Ariel Sharon was a highly controversial figure, to say the least, and a symbol of the humiliation the Palestinian people had endured for so long. Back in 1953, he commanded the Israeli military Unit 101, which carried out the infamous massacre at Qibya – a West Bank village located just five kilometres from Nabi Saleh. Sharon's troops entered the village on 14 October 1953, and killed at least 69 villagers, two-thirds of them women and children.[10]

This act was condemned widely, around the world. On 24 November 1953, the UN Security Council adopted Resolution 101 on the matter, expressing the "strongest possible censure of this action". Even The U.S. State Department demanded that the culprits should be brought to account. But nothing of that kind happened.

In 1973 Sharon was one of the founders of Israel's Likud Party, and some years later, as Israel's Minister of Defence he paid a visit to South African apartheid forces that were fighting the liberation movement SWAPO in South Africa-occupied Namibia.[11] In 1982, he led the Israeli invasion of Lebanon. This resulted in the Sabra and Shatila massacre that same September, when Lebanese far-right forces entered two Palestinian refugee camps which had been sealed off by the Israeli Army, and in cold blood slaughtered more than three thousand men, women and children under the eyes of the Israeli soldiers.[12]

This again led to an international outcry over Ariel Sharon. In Belgium, the High Court expressed the wish to try him for war crimes and genocide (although it was prevented from doing so because Sharon enjoyed the immunity of his office).[13]

The Second Intifada claimed thousands of Palestinian lives, and led to a series of suicide bombings which took the lives of hundreds of Israelis too.

Although Ahed grew up in time of enormous upheaval, she tried to be a child as every other child. She was particularly fond of playing football, and her dream was to become a professional football player. Quite unsurprisingly, her favourite subject at school has long been Physical Education/Sport.

But the military Occupation deprives the Palestinian children of their childhood. Ahed and her friends could be playing when the IDF soldiers would enter the village. "We were shocked when soldiers entered the places of play. They destroy all of our happiness," she told TeleSUR English.[14]

Ahed described her fear as a small child when soldiers came in the middle of the night to raid their home. By the time she was three, her father, Bassem, had been regularly carried away to so-called *administrative detention*, each time leaving the children in fear over what was going to happen to their father. Such an experience deprives a child of a basic feeling of safety.

The Israeli government also took the Second Intifada as an excuse to realise a plan presented by Prime Minister Yitzhak Rabin in 1992[15] to build a huge barrier separating the West Bank from Israel. The construction of this 708 kilometres long and 8 metres high wall, which cuts deep into the West Bank, began in 2002 and continued for several years. Here is not the place to go into detail of the disastrous humanitarian effects that the Wall has had on the lives of Palestinians – particularly in the field of health – but it also affected the lives of the Palestinian children. Many Palestinians have seen their homes destroyed and lost access to agricultural land, due to the wall.

Another problem is the Israeli military checkpoints. One such checkpoint controls the passage in and out of Nabi Saleh. "Sometimes", Ahed told TeleSUR English, "children go to amusement parks but all the fun is lost when they find the checkpoint is closed. We often come back from parties and find our way home barred by a closed checkpoint. I hope that the world's children never have to live such a difficult life."

The lives of the people in Nabi Saleh are also strongly affected by the presence of the Israeli settlement called Halamish, on the other side of a hill, just a few hundred metres away. Halamish, like other Israeli settlements is a gated community, strongly guarded by both the Army and armed settlers, erected on occupied land. The settlements began to be built immediately after the Israeli Occupation in 1967, and although declared illegal by the United Nations and several governments, they continue to be expanded.[16]

Halamish was created in October 1977, when a group of Israelis simply occupied the abandoned old Tegart Fort – a remnant from the British administrative rule in the 1930s – and declared it an Israeli settlement. The land that had belonged to the people of Nabi Saleh for centuries.

In 2008, when Ahed was seven and started school, events took a turn for the worse. That summer the settlers took control of the water spring of Ein el Qaws, located just on the outskirts of Nabi Saleh. This was a terrible blow to the villagers. The spring, owned by Ahed's father's uncle, Bashir Tamimi, was needed to irrigate hundreds of olive and fruit trees in the village. Ahed and the other children used to swim in it. But after the settlers occupied it, soldiers and armed settlers began to guard it, and when villagers tried to go to it, they were often prevented from doing so. The settlers were armed and very aggressive. They put up signs saying, "No Arabs allowed." The settlers also "solved" part of the problem with the irrigation of the villagers' olive trees by destroying all the olive trees at the spring.

Ahed's father, Bassem, played an important role, organising protest marches against the seizure of the spring. He had suffered heavily for his attempts to organise protests in the past, with imprisonment, even torture. When his sister, Basama, visited one of Bassem's trials at the military court in Ramallah, she was pushed down a staircase by an Israeli soldier. Her neck was broken; Bassem lost a sister, and five young children lost their mother.

Ahed grew up, fully aware of the fact that her aunt had been killed by the Occupation forces. But her father taught her not to hate. Bassem is a strong believer in non-violent protests. During the first demonstration against the seizure of the spring, he and the villagers held olive branches to show that it was a peaceful demonstration. But the Israeli Army met the demonstration with tear-gas grenades and rubber-coated steel bullets. The settlers had stood on the hill with their guns and watched happily as the Army used violence on the villagers, and then they too attacked the people. That Friday, they uprooted 153 of the olive trees that belonged to the villagers.

To Bassem, it is clear why the settlers act like this. "The settlers try to provoke us to commit acts of terrorism," he says, but firmly adds; "We will not allow ourselves to be provoked!" It is a message he emphasises:

"We want to create a successful model of civil protest, which will prove that we are not terrorists and that we are the owners of this land. We want to send a message to the Palestinian people and the Israeli people, that there is a different model of resistance, non-violent resistance. "[17]

This peaceful struggle led the villagers into contact with Israeli peace activists, who joined them. They began to gather once a week, every Thursday, in a park in Nabi Saleh. In this, particularly the women of Nabi Saleh and Israeli female peace activists came close together.

But the contrast with the armed settlers and the soldiers could not be greater. On several occasions, Ahed and her friends were unable to go to school because the Israeli military checkpoint which controls the entrance to the village was closed, and this of course had a negative effect on her studies.

The IDF's attempts to crush the protests has injured over a hundred villagers and cost the lives of many others, many from Ahed's family. In 2011, when Ahed was ten, an Israeli soldier shot her cousin Mustafa straight in the face with a high-velocity tear gas canister, blowing half his face off. Mustafa was rushed to hospital, but the doctors could not save his life. The next morning he died.

That same year, her father was again arrested and sent to prison. He was accused of "sending people to throw stones, and holding a march without a permit." Much of the world saw Bassem's imprisonment for what it was – an occupying army trying to clamp down on resistance. In 2012, Amnesty International declared Bassem a prisoner of conscience.

During long periods of her childhood, Ahed has had to take care of her little brothers when both of her parents were held in prison. Her mother, Nariman, has been arrested at least half a dozen times (at the time of writing, like Ahed, she has been in custody since December 2017). When TeleSUR English asked Ahed how it was, taking care of her little brothers and the home, in the absence of her parents, being so young herself, she said; "This is so hard, but I have to make myself strong and to appear happy, to not worry my little brothers. I have to wake them up in the morning, cook, do the homework, and look after them." She sighed and added, "My grades at school dropped when they arrested my mother."[18]

Ahed's life in an occupied zone is symbolised by the necklace she wears, which she made herself. The necklace contains used bullets she has found. This may seem strange, but Ahed explained: "We make beautiful things out of them, like jewellery. We create life from death. They came to kill us with it, but we convert it into things which we enjoy and benefit from." Shootings and death are all too real for Ahed; in 2012, when she was just 11 years old, her uncle, Rushdie Tamimi, was killed by the IDF soldiers. He was shot in his lower back with live ammunition.

Images of Palestinian children on demonstrations are used in Israeli propaganda with claims that they are used as *human shields*. But, in reality, the IDF recognises little difference between children and adults – witness Ahed's position as a prisoner in an Israeli military jail. There is no safe place for Palestinian children. Israeli soldiers often fire gas canisters through the windows into the houses, making it impossible to breathe, forcing entire families, children included, out onto the streets.

To an outsider, it is hard to imagine what a girl like Ahed has had to go through. It is even more difficult to understand how she can carry on without being swallowed by hatred. But of course, it is the result of the strong collective solidarity in the village, her upbringing, and the feeling that the cause of the villagers and the Palestinians is just. International solidarity, which in Ahed's and Nabi Saleh's case has multiplied in recent years, also plays an important role in enabling people around her to hold their heads high.

In terms of humanity it is important to see that many facets combine to make a character. Ahed is, of course, brave but it is perhaps in seeing Ahed's vulnerability that her bravery is to be fully admired. The American author Ben Ehrenreich spent a number of days in Nabi Saleh when Ahed was only 11 years old. In his excellent book, *The Way to the Spring: Life and Death in Palestine[19]*, he describes how Ahed, with her cousin and friend Marah, had been at the fore of a regularly held Friday march to the village spring when Israeli soldiers fired barrages of tear gas canisters at them. He writes:

> "The day the marchers made it to the spring and the soldiers chased her from the road Ahed was her usual stoic self but that night though she had nightmares, she talked in her sleep until morning, waking again in panic and fear."

Nevertheless, this is a fear that Ahed has, doubtlessly, had to wrestle with.

In trying to build a picture of Ahed I was grateful to Ben Ehrenreich's book on Palestine for his observations of Ahed as a younger child. The author name *Ehrenreich*, by the way, was totally familiar to me, from long before I had read his book. Just as Ben Ehrenreich had immersed himself in Palestinian life so his mother, Barbara, had delved into the life of the low paid waitresses and cleaners of America in her book, *Nickeled and Dimed*, from 2001[20]. As a lecturer at a Swedish university I had found that Barbara Ehrenreich's immersion into a life of poverty had often wrought empathy from the many students who chose to study it.

One of Ben Ehrenreich's descriptions of Ahed really jumps out at me. Nariman is combing the 11-year-old Ahed's hair, "Ahed, a thin, blond, slip of a girl, with her mother's bright green eyes." He continues, "She was reserved and almost always quiet, but she was not shy exactly. Even at rest something stayed taut in her, like a wire stretched along her spine." The description points to an alertness and sensitivity in the younger Ahed. Perhaps it is this *"tautness"* in Ahed which has prevented a meek submission to the Occupation.

In August that same year, 2012, Ahed came to the world's attention, when she was filmed, trying to save her mother from being arrested. The images show Ahed screaming and crying, trying to hug her mother, before being torn away from her by a group of heavily armed Israeli soldiers. The last scene shows her strongly held by a soldier, twice her size, while she hysterically cries for her mother. It is heart-wrenching to watch, and the video went viral, laying the ground for the image of Ahed Tamimi as a brave girl – although she perhaps only did what many children would have done in that situation.[21]

In another clip that went viral on YouTube at around the same time, Ahed is seen, devastated, after the soldiers have taken away her brother. (See qrcode 5 at the QR code section.)

> "Where have you taken him? Where have you taken him?" she screams at a soldier, her voice broken by tears. Ahed, her little brother, and a group of women challenge the large group of Israeli soldiers. Ahed tells them she is not afraid of them, or their weapons. "We will take our freedom", she says, "and if you cut down one olive tree, we will plant one hundred more!" When a French photographer, looking very frightened, is arrested by the soldiers and locked into a military vehicle, she tells him to not be afraid: "After every imprisonment there is freedom!"

The video, from August 2012, resulted in an invitation to Turkey to receive a prize for her courage. When meeting the then Prime Minister Erdogan, Ahed demonstrated not only bravery, but a strong sense of justice too. She challenged Erdogan, questioning why she, as a Palestinian had had to have a visa to enter Turkey, whereas Israelis required none.[22]

Ben Ehrenreich reveals a couple of other incidents involving Ahed which point to a more familiar picture of a child. He asked Ahed what she liked best about Turkey – she replied "The Sea", though it had been too cold to swim. Ehrenreich also points to an occasion when Ahed was feeling low – sad that she was not to have a 12th birthday party on her return home from Turkey. A universal desire for a party, recognisable to all children, though the cause of the party plans being put on ice is less familiar. Nariman, around this time, was in mourning because her brother, Rushdie, had been recently shot by the IDF. In her grief, Nariman had felt she could not face a party. But in an act familiar perhaps to all parents, given some time, the mother gave way to Ahed's wishes. Of course a 12-year-old girl should have a birthday party.

The protests against the seizure of the spring, and against the repression, continued. By 2017, they had held protest demonstrations every Friday for nearly a decade. In an article titled "Nabi Saleh is where I lost my Zionism," Lisa Goldman describes what she observed during a visit to the village:

> "Every week they gather at the top of the hill inside their village, carrying flags and banners, and walk toward the road that separates them from the spring. The goal is simply to cross the road and walk to the spring. And every week, the army deploys security forces inside and around the village to stop the protesters from reaching their destination.
>
> The way it works is this: at around noon, military vehicles enter the village and park at the bottom of its bisecting road. Security forces, heavily armed and wearing combat gear, descend from the vehicles, load their weapons, and wait. Sometimes they start shooting as soon as the demonstration begins, and sometimes they wait for a teenager to throw a stone in their direction before opening fire.
>
> As Ben Ehrenreich notes in his *New York Times Magazine* article about Nabi Saleh, the army spokesperson told him there has never been a single case of a soldier being injured by a stone at those demonstrations. But over the past few years, soldiers have injured and killed several demonstrators."[23]

When Ahed was fourteen, she again made headlines world-wide, although purely by accident. It all began with another attack by Israeli soldiers against a demonstration in Nabi Saleh. Ahed, her mother Nariman and Ahed's aunt Manal were at home. The mother was walking on crutches after having been shot in the leg with live ammunition a couple of months before. Gunfire and the popping of tear gas canisters being fired were heard. Suddenly the daughter of one of Ahed's cousins screamed out that the soldiers had taken Ahed's eleven-year brother Abu Yazan. Ahed and the women immediately rushed outside to come to the boy's rescue.

Abu Yazan, his arm broken and plastered in a sling, had been chased by a soldier. A viral video shows how the soldier grabs the boy, forces him to the ground so that he hits his face on a rock. In the next moment, Ahed and the women come to the boy's rescue. Screams of fear can be heard in the clip. The women do their best to free Abu Yazan, and in her desperation, Ahed bites the soldier's hand. Overpowered by the women and Ahed, the soldier loses his grip on Abu Yazan, who quickly gets on his feet and runs away to safety. Only one IDF soldier could come to support his colleague because the rest of the troops were busy apprehending Ahed's cousin and an Italian peace activist. It was a significant victory. The two IDF soldiers reluctantly conceded defeat but petulantly tossed a tear gas canister as they walked away.

When the film went viral, Ahed's renown spread even more around the world. She was interviewed on TV and her social media sites became incredibly popular. Many Palestinians began to embrace her as a symbol of a new generation standing up to Israeli rule. In 2016, Ahed was invited to the United States for a speaking tour titled "No Child Behind Bars/Living Resistance." She was denied a visa by the US authorities.

The Israeli cultural minister, Miri Regev, complained that the soldier whose hand had been bitten, should have been allowed to return fire (hardly a balanced equation). The idea was, of course, ridiculous.

The soldier's rifle was dangling in the face of Abu Yazan. Ahed had a tee shirt with a picture of the cartoon bird Tweetie Pie, and this added to the asymmetry of the situation. That a child should have been shot, for trying to save her brother simply served to expose the Occupation. Ahed was winning wide support internationally.

The Israeli right wing were beginning to see that Ahed was a thorn in their side. She received a growing number of threats on social media. Shortly after the release of the video, Ahed's 19-year-old brother Waed was arrested and imprisoned for ten months. When Ahed and Nariman were going to visit him in prison they were stopped at a checkpoint near Jerusalem. Israeli soldiers singled out Ahed, pulled her off the bus, and told her that she wouldn't be allowed to go any further.

For Ahed, harassment and fear became a way of life. In an interview with the UK's *Guardian* newspaper, in 2014, Ahed describes a 3am night raid: "I woke up, there were soldiers in my bedroom. My mum was screaming at the soldiers. They turned everything upside down, searching. They took our laptop and cameras and phones." Her house was even threatened with demolition. Ahed said she has been in clouds of tear gas too often to count. On its effects she says, "I can't breathe, my eyes hurt, it feels like I'm suffocating. Sometimes it's 10 minutes until I can see again.". All of this in stark contrast to the life that Ahed seemed to want to lead. *The Guardian* journalist pointed out that Ahed liked films about Mermaids and wanted to skip in the sitting room. She asked Ahed to stand near the watchtower at the entrance to Nabi Saleh for a photograph, but Ahed was nervous and clearly reluctant – getting away as quickly as possible.[24]

But Ahed defied her fear. Her mother has raised her to be strong, to demand her rights. That is what disturbs the Occupation regime and everyone that supports it; they would prefer to see Ahed grow up to be submissive.

*

Toward the end of our interview with Bassem, I reflect on all he told us and asked how he was coping, with a wife and daughter in prison.

> "At the moment its complex, when I go to see Ahed I see she is a bit empty and her mother a bit empty, it's a sad moment. When I want to make food for the children – sad moment. When we sit to eat – sad moment. When we made the birthday for Ahed it was a very sad moment."

Ahed became 17 in prison on 31 January of this year (2018) and so her birthday was celebrated by her family at her home – in her absence. Bassem continued:

> "Every moment is a sad moment. I am worried because I have experience from military prison. I am worried when she comes to the military court because I recall what happened to my sister inside the military court. I am worried when Ahed is in interrogation because I personally nearly died after 14 days of that. I worry about all the propaganda created in the media against Ahed. I worry too that two days ago someone came into our own village and wrote graffiti saying that they want to kill Ahed, that they want to drive the Tamimi family from the land. I worry also because she loses her childhood."

In Shakespeare's play *Macbeth*, the warrior-lord Macduff, upon hearing the news of his family's murder, breaks down and cries, and his fellow comrades ask him why he weeps when he should fight. Macduff replies that he *shall* fight like a man, but he must also *feel* it like a man. Similarly, Bassem caught up in this liberation struggle, with his family on the line, is strong enough to show vulnerability, as he redoubles his determination. I sit with him and see how his body hunches a little, his eyes narrow, and glaze once more. But I feel he will recover from the blows of the unshared meals, the birthday parties that pass by… the childhood interrupted, and the family torn apart. He continues:

"She has become responsible for something I and everyone in the world must be responsible for. Who must slap the face of this occupying army? Not Ahed alone surely? Everyone in the world who believes in the human value of the human life. But also I feel proud. She is very strong, she can help give confidence to others. She can solve any problem that she faces. I think everyone, every father in the world would like their daughter to be like her – to stand bravely in front of an armed man, who has occupied your country, invaded your garden. For that I feel proud, I feel lucky that she is like this, but also some politicians and media are blaming us as parents – saying that we don't like our children or that we exploit them, all of that."

Bassem suggests that in his position as a parent he does not have a real choice. That people who criticise him as a parent are not living like he does, as a second class citizen, under the boot of an occupier. He says "The soldiers come anyway, however I raise my children." Bassem feels that if he as a father had rather discouraged Ahed from fighting back they would both have paid a heavy price. He says "She perhaps wouldn't dare to go out, can't go out, she will be broken psychologically, she will be destroyed." Bassem feels that in order to survive "she must participate", participate in the liberation movement. He stresses that Ahed could not simply be hidden at home, away from trouble. That she has to go to school and then she walks past an armed soldier from another country, a soldier protecting people who are stealing her land, and even the water. He says the option of *not* fighting to be free now…

"…is unrealistic. We cannot wait for America or a European nation to promise that everything will be OK in 10 years' time and that, yes, maybe then I can send Ahed to be a dancer. We haven't the choice, we must encourage our children to be strong. From the beginning, from when we started our struggle, we said that the role of the women is the cornerstone for the movement. Three strong women of different ages in the family might mean three strong generations who are better able to struggle. Ahed, like every child has had a dream but she is absolutely determined and won't accept losing dignity and freedom. I see how she understands."

Bassem suggests he and Ahed share an understanding of the essence of the problems they face. That is, that the problem is not just the *physical* Occupation and the actual settlement on their land but the *mentality* of the Occupation. The problem they are dealing with, at its core, is in the *mentality* of colonisation. "It is this mentality which must change if we want to change the future." Bassem is somewhat in awe of Ahed's ability to have grasped this concept at a young age.

> "Once when Ahed was 13, a European journalist asked her if she could imagine playing together with the Israeli settler children, in the water of the spring, which the settlers had illegally taken. Ahed had replied; *Yes if they accept to live with the same rights and equality, but I can't accept that anyone has power over me, to control my life.*"

The Israeli right wing politicians and media are determined that such intelligence and insight from Ahed is not permitted to be seen by the world. They want to present a stereotypical, one-sided picture of Ahed. Some referred to her as Shirley Temper (a play on the American child actor from the 1950s, Shirley Temple). Israel's deputy Minister Michael Oren preposterously suggested that the Tamimi family were paid actors (in this context Palestine is referred to as *Pallywood*).[25] Here, Michael Oren is a victim of his own racism or stereotyping – for him it is impossible for Palestinians to have blue eyes or fair hair.

*

The interview was over. Bassem agreed to meet us later in the afternoon and drive with us to the village, he assured us that, at the moment, there were no checkpoints.

Later, at 3pm, Bassem arrived punctually, as arranged. This time he had a couple of plastic bags of shopping with him, he had bought something for the two sons he had at home. With Nariman in jail, he was living as a single parent. We walked down the High Street having to stop occasionally as Bassem was greeted by people he knew. The Ramallah streets were busy and the sun was shining, it was over 20 degrees, strangely hot for February according to Bassem, "This time last year we had snow."

Two weeks later, on 13 February, the date of Ahed's next court hearing, the weather would be wintery grim, misty and bitterly cold. An appropriate framing for the military prison and court at Ofer, Jerusalem.

I was glad to have Bassem's directions and knowledge to steer our car away from the congested centre. Soon we were winding through the hilly backstreets and the outer suburbs of Ramallah, its white or yellowing concrete bright in the sun. We passed Birzeit University on the edges of Ramallah as the town opened to countryside; a campus that seemed to offer some ambition in its scale and spread, but it looked faded and run-down. Run-down like almost all that we saw in the West Bank, apart from some shops in Central Ramallah which were trying to capture commerce's glitter. There was even a Kentucky Fried Chicken restaurant, a KFC, which even offered a history on the wall, like a timeline, of itself, with the date marked of its own "revolutionary" arrival in Palestine. No other history was mentioned, like liberation struggles, or Intifadas, as if these meant nothing compared to its own business.

But the name Birzeit University felt far removed from such a move to depoliticise or commercialise the West Bank. I recalled the name *Birzeit University* from my own time in British student politics some thirty years before, when, at the UK National Union of Students' conferences, resolutions would be moved to twin with Birzeit University students and demand an end to the Israeli Occupation, to move forward to a twin state solution. Bassem had been at the university too and the hope was that Ahed would go there one day, on her way to becoming a lawyer.

Out in the countryside, with the window of the car open and the warm air rushing through, I was struck by the grandeur and scale of the land. The hills were bigger, the valleys wider than I imagined. The landscape felt a little greener than I had expected too... I had dwelt on the stones in the histories I had read. The rocks and stones have taken on symbolic proportions as they are the main physical weapon of protest against the Occupation, an unarmed protest against a military might.

The sweeps of the bends, their sudden sharp turns and climbs, reminded me of holiday drives in the Scottish highlands, but this time with a warm Mediterranean twist. I had been in the icy, snowy white of Sweden a few days before and would be heading back there soon too. The contrast was remarkable and impacted strongly on me. I couldn't help but think of this area in a time of peace, with tourists and roadside cafés and vineyards.

But I couldn't relax too much. I thought of how we would drive back to East Jerusalem in the dark, me and Paul, our phones full of photos and interviews – our notebooks filled with Tamimi references and mail addresses. Would we get stopped? I thought of the graffiti which had appeared on a wall in Nabi Saleh calling for death to Ahed and revenge for the IDF. Bassem had mentioned it, and I had read of it in the Israeli newspaper, *Haaretz*. Tension was high. We were in an occupied zone. Young and twitchy Israeli conscripts had their fingers on the triggers of Mi6 rifles. Before travelling I had read of Rachel Corrie, an American student who had gone to the Palestinian Gaza Strip as part of a twinning arrangement with her college and had joined a protest against demolitions. She had been run over by an armoured bulldozer driven by a soldier. I thought of how I needed to get back to my family. I recalled the anxious look on my wife's face when I had said I wanted to go to the West Bank. Anders, the friendly driver of the little school bus who came and picked up my autistic son every day had warned me: "Watch your back!"

I was pulled back to a summer feeling by the sight of a balloon, like a large hot air balloon, calm and high in the shimmering heat haze of the distant sky. Perhaps the locals could just be enjoying this special early summery day. Perhaps I needed to relax. I pointed out the balloon. "That's the army observation balloon above our village." commented Bassem. "It has cameras."

Tension time again. We passed the Israeli illegal settlement of Halamish, with its high metal gates, and an army base nearby to protect them. Bassem seemed to tense a little, though not as much as me and Paul. He was used to it. His description of there being no checkpoints on the way had made me think I would see no soldiers but as we neared his village of Nabi Saleh there was a military watchtower, a permanent feature; it made me gasp inside. It was like a grey, foreboding lighthouse. Dark strengthened glass circled its top… and it was ringed with barbed wire. I imagined the soldiers were watching us come in. We stopped to photograph the recent death-to-Ahed Graffiti, now scrawled over by the local youth, determined to have the last word.

We drove on and pulled up outside a house at the end of a row of houses, quite big detached houses with almost a villa (if slightly ramshackle) feel to them. The houses were built on slopes… steps of stones led down to the gardens, the verandas of the backs of the houses looked out across a valley and the rise of the next slopes where the Israeli settlement was. Above all this loomed the balloon, still, watching.

The warmth of the afternoon had begun to thin and chill, the brightness dampening to grey. The lateness of the day, the ebbing away of the warmth, and above all – the close military presence, pressed in like a growing claustrophobia. The small road in, past the watchtower, the hovering balloon, all made me feel like we had driven into a trap. Indeed, the village can often be sealed off by the military. I was already worried about getting out of there in the dark.

This apprehension would not last long, as friendly faces came out of a house to greet us. Some of them I had read about or seen on the internet. Here was Bilal, Bassem's brother, he was polite and even a little shy. Just as Ben Ehrenreich had described him so charmingly in his book – like a friendly maths teacher. He seemed clever, reassuringly wise. With his YouTube documentation, he is the curator of Nabi Saleh. Here was his wife too, Manal. I had seen her from a video about Palestinian super-mums on Al Jazeera and YouTube. I knew I was walking into a crucial living history. Eyes from much of the world were on this village. Nabi Saleh was looked to, as a source of hope, by the growing numbers supporting Ahed and many long engaged with the Palestinian struggle.

We had walked past an array of tear gas canisters as we went into the home of Bilal and Manal. They were hanging in the garden, on a wire mesh, where another family might have a plant weaving through the holes. And inside as we went into the hall on a cabinet was a collection of tear gas canisters of varying sizes where you might expect to see ornaments or photographs. This was a house under siege.

Bassem went off to his house up the road and asked us to come along later. We sat down in the front room, got introduced to Bilal and Manal's children, a teenage girl, offered her hand. This was their only daughter, Rand, polite and somehow out of place in this war-like zone, and Samer, their youngest son, equally polite, buzzing about with a happy child's energy. The other sons, Mohammad and Osama were in prison. Manal told us Mohammad had been taken from this very home, in the night. Osama, had been plucked by the soldiers from a taxi at the watchtower, where a checkpoint had been established at the entrance to the village. Manal told me the taxi driver wasn't local and hadn't known which house Osama was from, and hadn't told them of the arrest. The IDF said nothing and the family had searched for over 24 hours for him before the lawyer, Gaby Lasky, was able to get news of him, in a military jail.

The soldiers often came in the house at night. At other times they were content to shower the house with skunk water, stinking and putrid. Water cannon is often seen on TV news but the water cannon of the IDF did not spray water, and TV screens cannot convey the stink of it. The IDF purchased a special chemical concoction for their water cannon. The locals seemed to prefer to call it *shit water*. Its smell could stay on the skin of a human or the outside of a building for days… demanding scrubbing and scrubbing.

Bilal asked us to sit on the sofa and served us with little cups of strong Arabic coffee. Then, a face, familiar from the internet, came in the room. It was the youngest journalist in the world, Janna Jihad (Janna's name *Jihad*, by the way, means simply *exertion* in Arabic and can be used in a variety of contexts… not just war-like ones). I had seen her on YouTube and on Facebook, where she has a quarter of a million followers, talking very confidently in amazingly strong English for an 11-year-old. A month after my visit I am pleased to report that Janna received an official journalist card and accreditation from the Palestinian authorities (in March 2018).

I went to interview Janna whilst Paul stayed to interview Manal. Bilal, modestly, had deferred to his wife saying Manal spoke so much more articulately than him.

In another airy lounge-like room, Janna sat on a sofa beneath two posters, one demanding the release of Ahed, the other, the release of Mohammad. Janna seemed witty and spirited, healthy and energetic. Nawal, her mum sat on the adjacent sofa, she emanated pride.

I ask if Janna can describe what has happened to Ahed:

"She was arrested…by the Israeli military Occupation soldiers…

they came at 3am…just for trying to protect the children that was playing near her house because the soldier wanted to go to her house because her house is in a high area to shoot …"

Janna uses her hands to explain the military style logistics of this – she is 11 years old! I think about her lost childhood too.

"…To shoot on the children that were playing near her house, so she didn't let them and she was arrested for about, like, two months … like more…and it's like really bad."

Me: "And Mohammad, also on a poster, what's the situation with him?"

"Mohammad is my first cousin. He was arrested on 11 January 2018, kept till now, we don't know the reason…the police station is a very bad place. They hit him and it makes problems with him, he was isolated for 20 or more days. They didn't let him wear thick clothes…and they put the air conditioner on very cold and they didn't let him eat much…it's a very bad situation there."

I try to get a feel if there was a more normal childhood that I might recognise. I ask if she could remember playing with Ahed and if she had some stories of times together.

Janna smiles her wide and relaxed smile and says "Yeah till now we play. We play hide and seek, we play sometimes catch, and…" and Janna makes a big long list of child games, peppered with Arabic terms (I later asked an Arabic speaking friend and I learnt the list included hopscotch and jump). In fact, despite the military presence there is something old-fashioned in Nabi Saleh in that the kids do play out. Me and Paul meet many of the children later, boys and girls, playing football in the dark together (Janna amongst them).

I ask Janna how she would like to be living life with Ahed, when they are older, if she could choose:

"I wanna be living like everybody in the world in peace, and love, and equality, and justice. Living my childhood, not seeing my friends getting arrested or getting killed, not seeing my brother getting injured or my mum getting arrested...and my friends being in jail...live like any child in the world...go to the sea. Live my life in freedom, get my rights."

I stop at this point about going to the sea and mention that I know that Ahed likes the sea.

"I only went the sea once in my life with a school trip to Haifa. The Israeli occupying soldiers don't let us reach the sea or swim in the sea...it's really hard."

I ask if Ahed has been to the sea.

"She only went once, when she was about ten years old."

Me: "Can you see the ocean from here?"

"We can see it...from the roof... it's not very far but we cannot go to it."

The checkpoints stood in the way, only very occasionally open for travel to the sea.

This paradox of the sea's close proximity and its inaccessibility jolts me. I find myself reflecting on it over the days and weeks after I meet Janna. Inevitably we hear other's accounts through our own culture and experience. I think of my own childhood holidays by the sea. I studied as a schoolboy a Charles Dickens' novel *Dombey and Son,* where a seriously ill child is taken to the sea as a source of potential recovery. The child is fascinated by the waves, loves to be near them, to hear the sound and the rhythm. Perhaps Dickens comes to my mind because he usually writes of a world often unable, or unwilling, to provide a quality childhood. I had paid a fleeting visit to the fairly luxurious beach at Tel Aviv just a few days before, just to stand for a brief moment near the waves, to try and shake out the chills of a Swedish winter. To have then arrived in land-locked (for the Palestinians) Ramallah was to enter a modern tale of two cities. The life of a child from the nearby settler village, free to move through checkpoints to the sea, was far from the restricted Palestinian childhood.

I ask Janna about Ahed's reading.

> "She likes the fantasy books, classic books, adventures… she reads a lot…she loves the big books like those that have 400, 500 pages…"

Music?

> "Yeah we like pop music, we like rap… a song named Panda, La La by Shakira, most of Shakiras's songs, Rhianna's songs…".

Here, as with her answer about play and games, Janna has to pepper her list with Arabic names and I am simply unable to catch them. I do know that Janna and Ahed danced and acted to a version of *La La* by Shakira, and tens of thousands had seen their performance on You-Tube. The IDF even made (unbeknown to them) an appearance in the Video as Ahed ran up to a few soldiers and gave them the red card, this after she kicked a gas canister into touch!

In, for me, more familiar territory, I ask about Ahed and football and discover that Ahed plays in the midfield and likes Barcelona and Neymar. Later Bassem tells me that Ahed has a signed shirt from Neymar. I am reminded that Ahed had been forced to put away childhood dreams and change ambition– from footballer to lawyer. Janna said:

> "From when she was small she wanted to be a lawyer to support the prisoners, the children prisoners, to let all the Palestinian prisoners out from Israeli prisons and to protect them."

I heard too that Janna and Ahed had been to a conference in South Africa last summer to spread the word about their struggle. (The flight abroad only possible with a circuitous route to Jordan, rather than the nearby Tel Aviv airport.) Here, on a lighter note, Janna shared a story about when they both went to a shopping mall… Ahed had needed to tie her shoe laces and rested her foot on the rail of a car – only for the driver to beep the horn loudly. Janna smiles at the recollection of the surprise which presumably had led to a giggly escape. But Janna clearly knew too the significance of the trip to South Africa; I was struck by the extent of her insight at such a young age as she told me about how they had played a part in spreading a message of their plight around the world.

I was curious how she had got so good at English and she was full of praise for her school. "So you want to be a journalist?" I asked. I was bowled over by her enormously enthusiastic and ambitious reply:

> "Actually I want to be five things. Firstly, I want to study political science so I know more about the governments of the world. Secondly, I want to be a journalist, of course Palestine will be free in those days…"

(Serendipitously, birdsong comes through the window at this point – really!)…

> "I will cover the things that happen to all the children in the world. Thirdly, I want to be an artist to draw everything that I imagine and make this message go to the people in a nicer way. Fourth, I wanna be a fashion designer to design more of the Palestinian traditional dresses and make it fit the fashion for those years. Fifth, and last thing, I want to be a football player, with Barcelona, to write my country's name high."

As I had interviewed Janna, her mum, Nawal, was in the room. I asked her too if I could ask a few questions. She was obviously proud of her remarkable daughter – but I also asked her about her own life here. She told me about the night raids and how hard it was for her elderly mother, Fadwa, aged 74. Fadwa was ill with kidney troubles, but still had to get out of bed when the soldiers came at 3 or 4am, as they often did. Janna sometimes filmed the night raids but the soldiers sometimes deleted the film. Janna does, however, manage to broadcast live on Facebook from the village often. A reminder that digital technology could definitely help to make the Occupation a thing of the past.

But right now the Occupation was hurting the people of the village. Nawal complained that a half hour trip to the Ramallah hospital, for her mother to receive dialysis for her kidney complaint, could take over two hours if the check points were in place. She pointed too to the bars and wire mesh on the windows, to stop the tear gas canisters being shot into the house; windows were protected in all the houses.

I asked Janna if she could take me to meet more of Ahed's friends and cousins. She suggested I meet Nour and Marah. As we stepped out of the hallway I asked about the collection of tear gas canisters by the door – in the front garden. She told me that they had managed to collect enough to make a giant work of art of with them, like an exhibition of masses of small canisters hung on a mesh, with a Palestinian flag. In typical resilient fashion she declared that they could make something positive out of the things that could kill them.

Mustafa Tamimi, Janna's cousin, was killed not so far from the spot where we stood. Killing and death and blood are so often the language of hyperbole, but when Janna uses these terms, it is with a literal meaning, a reality almost beyond my comprehension. She is eleven years old and talks of killings she has seen, and whilst she is angry, the familiarity is so strong for her the tales flow in an almost blasé manner – a manner which suggests she has witnessed more cruelty than she ought to have.

I ask her about skunk water too. Luckily, she is able to laugh about the liquid concoction… It smells of "vomit, rotten eggs, and stinky socks". Her description makes me think of the army as akin to a school bully armed with stink bombs. I can't help but feel Janna represents a more civilized future and that history will laugh at these bullies just as the former East German leader Honecker was mocked at the fall of the Berlin Wall, or how Charlie Chaplin ridiculed Hitler and Mussolini.

Janna takes me up the road to another house, to meet Nour and Marah. On the way I see a boy riding bare back on a donkey, past the petrol station, a strange sight for me and I know that I am far from home, in rural Palestine. I had never been here before and it felt so different from my home, not only the obvious difference of a donkey as an actual means of transport (not just a fun ride on a beach), but also the village itself was different to my reality. The houses were built on terraces, on a steep hillside and looking up was that most incongruous thing of all – the balloon with the cameras. Would something spark an incident and would the soldiers from the watchtower at the entrance to the village steam in? Would we be caught up in something, shot even? The fear of the Occupation again. I once again seriously considered that we would be stopped on the way out of the village at the watchtower and the IDF would see our notes and look at our phones... and remove everything.

But the cheerfulness of Nabi Saleh snapped me out of my gloom. It seemed, despite the Occupation, a happy place. I was reminded of a childhood holiday to Ireland, going round as a kid in a gang of other kids. For there were lots of kids out and about, playing cheerfully. "What's your name?" I would be asked by a group of boys playing football in the street. We stopped a while and chatted – "Which team do you support?" The international language of football.

We turned a corner and approached another roomy garden and villa. Nour and Marah's family were sat out on a terrace enjoying the last of the evening, on plastic chairs – a few of them smoking. Someone had rang ahead and the father of the house, Naji, came forward to welcome us. The extended family gathering were all friendly, though I felt I was interrupting a cosy chat. There were three generations there I guessed, grandparents, parents, and a toddler, and a baby. Indeed I felt a little like another symbol of this interrupted life they had. It could have been rural France in springtime, a villa on a hill, enjoying a rich peaceful life. But it was Palestine and settlers wanted their land and water – and they had an army to harass them away. I'd already met a mum in the village earlier, whose husband had left for America. If you were not going to fight and fight and fight, and then, when you were more than exhausted by the night raids and the gas, and the threat of demolition, fight some more, you would, eventually, leave. That, presumably, was what the illegal settlers wanted; that was what the occupying army wanted too, to make life so uncomfortable that you would just give up and go.

I met Nour, and it was clear, she wasn't running away in a hurry at all. I had seen her too on the internet, she had been in the viral YouTube incident with Ahed and the two soldiers. Nour too had been arrested. I had seen her on the internet on her release from prison. She was a few years older than Ahed, studying journalism.

I asked her about the incident which went viral on YouTube. She had been there with Ahed when they tried to get rid of the soldiers from the driveway.

> "I was at home and heard sounds from Ahed's house so I went there to see what was happening. I saw the soldier inside the property and my cousins were filming them…I was just there for an hour and then the Israeli soldiers started shooting rubber bullets…"

They are actually steel bullets with a rubber coating.

> "…and tear gas and everything, so one of my cousins was shot by a rubber bullet in his face, Mohammad, and he had been taken to the hospital and it had been dangerous for him so when

we heard that, we felt like we have to make the soldiers go away from the house…but they said that they have to stay there and that they could do what they wanted. We replied 'No – this is our house and we have the right to tell you to go away.' They started to try to make us go away but when they saw that we were filming they made out they were peaceful. We pushed them to go away from the house but nothing happened, they went away at the end of the day. We went back in the house and then to the hospital to see Mohammad…they came to arrest Ahed and I expected that they would arrest me too but they decided to take Ahed first. They took her to prison and then they took me the next night, at 3 o' clock in the morning. It was very hard, you know, you don't know where you are going, you don't know what is happening. This is the first time for us – we've never been arrested before."

It feels so strange hearing this story from Nour. She seems so calm, she sits in a comfortable, modern front room on a fairly lavish settee, and yet she tells me these tales of being on the wrong end of a military Occupation. It's as if my mind struggles to match the tale of a brutal Occupation with such well-educated and civilised company. I listen intently.

"So… we go to the police station. I think I was 18 hours at the police station. They don't let me sleep. When I try to sleep they scream and bang the table to make me wake up… and nothing to eat, if you are thirsty you have to ask a lot of times to get a glass of water. So, it was like they push us to give information about all of our family, about the video they ask me everything about the video – about Ahed, my aunt (Nariman), about every person who was in the video and they say to me that if I don't tell them everything they will come to my house and arrest my father. I was always silent, just saying 'I don't know what happened' because I knew they would take the words from my mouth if I say any words.

And then in the middle of the night they take me to Hasharon Prison in the Borstar (an armoured car). It's very cold, they turn the air conditioning down or off. Then we go to Hasharon prison. It's hard, the situation of the girls there is bad. They are sick and it's hard. About the court – I was there a long time and then at 2am they take me from Hasharon to Ofer Jail (because the court is there) and then they took me back. They make me suffer. It was hard for me...from this time I have suffered from this incident, I have court hearings, there is a lot of things I have to do- my life has changed you know."

When I listen to Nour and compare with interviews Manal Tamimi has given about her arrest I actually wonder if Nour is trying to suppress or forget some of the worst of her experiences from custody.[26] Manal describes being in a cage like structure with an aggressive Israeli criminal held adjacently, who was trying to grab Nour, Manal and Ahed whilst the soldiers looked on, laughing.

As I ended my interview with Nour, in came Ahed's friend and classmate, Marah. *Came in* feels an understatement – Marah bounded in and I felt her enthusiasm and energy. She was dressed in sporty, youthful clothes, trainers and looked ready to go to the gym. Marah and Ahed spent a great deal of time together and I guessed I could learn a deal about Ahed from Marah. They had known each other from when they were very young and had played together from their earliest years. I asked if Marah could tell me about when Ahed was very young. Marah laughed and said: "She was not nervous and when she said she would do something she really did it!"

Me: "What were her favourite subjects in school?"

Here Marah laughed as if there was only one possible answer. Indeed, the answer was familiar.

Marah: "Sport. Ahed loves football!"

I asked where she played, her position in a team.

Marah: "Everywhere!" (Again with laughter).

Me: "Is she good at football?"

Marah: "Yes!"

Again we get a confirmation that Barcelona is the favourite team, shared with much laughter. Marah liked Messi whereas Ahed liked Neymar (I got the impression that the admiration would survive his move to the Paris club, PSG). I asked Marah seriously if she thought Ahed could become a professional football player. Once again, I heard of the diversion to a legal fight.

Marah: "She had thought that she could become a player but when the demonstrations began she decided to study to be lawyer... because she wants to send a message to the world."

I asked Marah, if she could send a message to Ahed in prison, what it would be. Despite our interview having been light-hearted (Nour had translated and they had laughed warmly between them over some recollections), the tone became profound now.

> "Stay strong and take care... we are alright and we are proud of you."

By now I was reunited with Paul (he had interviewed Manal Tamimi) and we walked up the hill to Bassem's house. Now we were walking to where the soldiers had met the determined Ahed and Nour, some 6 weeks earlier.

It was night now, and me and Paul were anxious to head back to Jerusalem. We were thinking of checkpoints and all that could happen. It was to be a fairly quick visit to Bassem's house if Bassem didn't mind.

We approached the driveway to Ahed's family home, near the exact ground where Ahed had demanded that the soldiers leave. A track went round the front of the house. Beyond the track, the land dropped off. In the darkness I couldn't see how steep the drop was, or how far down it went. On the other side of the valley was the settlers' illegal village – and somewhere out there was the military tower and the soldiers' base. It seemed, in the darkness as if Ahed's house stood on the edge of a precipice.

When we came into Bassem's front room, a number of men from the village were sat on the sofa, in a hushed conference. The tone was sombre, but we were greeted in a warm and friendly way. Bassem had perhaps said that we were on our way, that we were writing this book. There were no women present. Ahed and Nariman were of course in prison. There were no youngsters either, Bassem's two younger sons, were perhaps out at play. Bassem offered us tea or coffee and I declined – jokingly suggesting the strong coffee was giving me the shakes. I had attempted to lighten the tone, but I was reminded of the seriousness of the matters at hand when Bassem, introduced me to Fadel, Mohammad's father. There were actually a lot of Mohammads in the village (most of them used nicknames, like Bassem's son Abu Yazan, another Mohammad). Fadel's boy was the 15 -year-old Mohammad who had had to have an operation on his brain. Who had been put into an induced coma after the rubber coated steel bullet had gone through his face, at close range. The 15 -year-old Mohammad, whose injuries – their grimness and freshness – had so fired up Ahed on that fateful December day.

I offered some sort of condolences in my respectful nodding to Mohammad's father. I knew only too well his fears. I have been trained as a teacher to deal with pupils with head injuries. In England the pupils I had worked with had had their injuries from car crashes not bullets, but I knew what could follow a severe head injury. It wasn't just the physical scars. There could be the loss of memory, a possible change in personality, a potential to say inappropriate things, and worst of all perhaps – the possible difficulty in keeping hard earned friendships. One might almost become someone else. I had seen the *before and after* the shooting pictures of Mohammad. The effects of the shooting were clearly brutal; it looked like a piece of his head was missing.

The doctors planned much and would no doubt restore the skull, and Nabi Saleh seemed a loving place, if under siege, – hope and optimism would have to be clung on to for Mohammad. What else could be done?

But a few weeks after my meeting with Fadel, Mohammad's father, on the night of 25 February 2018, the village was raided by the IDF, and Mohammad, a patient who ought to be convalescing, kept warm and relaxed, was arrested in the middle of the night. They came for 9 others too from Nabi Saleh; Manal Tamimi interviewed on Al Jazeera called the raid particularly violent. The tear gas was fired, the vile stinking skunk water was sprayed on people and houses, and arrests were made. The patient, Mohammad Tamimi, 15 years old, with his tender, broken head, awaiting skull restorative surgery, was interrogated and kept for a whole day. General Yoav Mordechai, Israel's Coordinator of Activities in the Territories wrote on 27 February that Momamed's injuries were caused by the handlebars of a bike, after an accident. However, journalists had seen Mohammad's CAT scan and images of "the bullet fractures removed from his skull."[27] The Occupation was not only vicious in terms of repression, it was clearly vicious in terms of its capacity to lie too. However, the distortion of the truth was so wild that it is easy to sense the bankruptcy of the Occupation – a rottenness way beyond reason or rationality.

After a short while sat in Bassem's lounge, most of the men left and I asked Bassem if I could film him in Ahed's bedroom for this book. He took me in and showed me her latest piece of school work, her award for courage from Turkey and a photo from her South African speaking tour, and a football poster. Despite these objects in the room, the most striking feature of the bedroom was the emptiness. There was a cuddly toy there, and a few pictures, but the room was now unused, unslept in, and the weight of the absence seemed to rest heavily on Bassem.

Here had the police come, in the middle of the night. Ahed was gone. The bedroom was still, like a photograph kept for a memory.

Back in the lounge, a friend of Bassem's took some pictures of us: Bassem, Paul and me – holding an Ahed placard from Amnesty International, with the proud boast of over a million signatures on the #FreeAhed petition. But Ahed was still locked up, as was her mother Nariman, along with the thousands of other Palestinians, hundreds of them children, in Israeli military jails.

Before we left Bassem, he held our hands briefly, even gave us a light peck on the cheek. I took it as a sign that we had come close to him and that he was giving us some trust, and hoped we would not let him down. He had lost so much, yet what he wanted to win was not unreasonable. His daughter, his wife – he wanted them back, and he wanted his land. He had lost his sister.

And Bassem knew a lot about facts. He had earlier, in our interview, referred to one of the founders of the scientific method, Francis Bacon, from 1600s England. Bassem's resistance was shaped by the *fact* of Israel's Occupation, as solidly as Bacon's method was rooted in a search for facts, using empiricism, in an age of reason.

Bassem had instilled in his daughter a sense of right – but it was not without sacrifice, he was worried that she might pay dear for that.

As me and Paul drove away, unstopped, from the military watchtower at the edge of Nabi Saleh, we let out a sigh of relief (though we knew we might still have other military checkpoints to come). The evening was late now, moonless and blackening as we left the village, far from city lights. Bassem might have been calling his two young sons to come in, perhaps eating together as a family, with what he had bought from Ramallah earlier. 11-year-old Salam and 14-year-old Abu Yazan would later go to bed, without a mother or sister at home. During the weeks ahead, the nights in their little village would be penetrated by the bangs of guns shooting tear gas, and the stink of the skunk water. The Occupation would trundle through the village, loudly; in effect, urging the villagers to leave – emigrate – give up. The dreams of Bassem's sons would perhaps be filled with dread, turning to nightmares, under the harassment. A nightmare they might wake from, only to see a living military nightmare played out, outside their window. They might imagine their friends being dragged from their houses. Perhaps too, like Ahed when she was younger, they might not be able to return to sleep, but at least Ahed had had her mother to turn to. It was a grim scene in my mind. Nabi Saleh under siege at night. As Bassem had said to me earlier that day – the Occupation is based on fear.

Ahed's room would lie empty, an evocation of a girl's or young woman's life, interrupted.

I had been on a journey of discovery about Ahed. Like any other girl she had wanted to play, and when she was young there were lots of games. She had her friends and her reading, her music and dancing too. She had had nightmares too, more real than any child's should be. And she had had to be brave and stand up to her enemy. She had had to put away hopes and dreams of being a footballer and decided that in this land, occupied by another land, she would have to choose a profession to help those around her. So Ahed had chosen to study to be a lawyer.

Bassem, when we interviewed him, assured us that, at that point, in early February, Ahed had company, with some peers, in prison. He said she was understandably a little shy of the media attention, but that she mixed well with the other political prisoners. There was always a fear of solitary confinement – that threat hung over all of the hundreds of child prisoners in Israel. But for now she could mix with others and continue with her studies in prison too. Bassem proudly reported that earlier prisoners had won the right to study, even take exams, after a hunger strike.

The hunger strike victory serves to remind us that Bassem is a seasoned campaigner. He has also now been served an international travel ban, as the Israeli leaders know he is a persuasive orator. It is an enormous tribute to Ahed, that Bassem, with his wealth of experience in the resistance movement, sees her not only as a daughter, but as a worthy comrade who stands alongside him in a struggle for freedom. Bassem told us about when he translated Ahed's speech to a large gathering:

> "When we were in South Africa last summer, we saw the radiance of resistance. Ahed saw a lot of tears, everyone was crying, there were hundreds, 7 or 800 people. She stood up and said 'Thanks for your tears.' …This is part of what I see. How she is and this gives me a spirit for this generation. How they touch this thing. She said… 'Thank you for your tears but we have a lot of tears because of tear gas and I don't want you to feel sad for my issue, my dignity is from my homeland and my people. For dignity's sake I don't want sadness for me, or for you to feel pity for me. I would like you to see me as a freedom fighter not a victim. When you see me as a freedom fighter this means that you can support me in a real way, how we supported you before [during Apartheid]. We don't mean for you to see us as a victim, to send some money, we don't need your money, you have a lot of poor in your country, you can give your money to your poor.'… She touched the main point in the struggle and the whole idea. I understand the theory, but maybe she touches the *main* idea."

Bassem feels hope for the future, symbolised by Ahed and the young generation.

Me and Paul had got through the checkpoints. We had driven through the checkpoint into East Jerusalem, from the West Bank, unstopped (I had noticed in my rear view mirror that the car behind was stopped). We had taken a long way round to make it look like we were tourists coming from the Dead Sea. And now I had passed through the questions at the airport.

I bought a coffee and browsed my phone and the *Haaretz* webpage. The Israeli police said they had enough evidence to charge Prime Minister Netanyahu with corruption, of taking bribes on an enormous scale; even his most loyal supporters had turned on him. Only a week earlier at the airport in Sweden, when flying out, I had bought copy of *The Economist* magazine with a front page boasting of an interview with Netanyahu, like he was someone they were so proud to be talking to. In it, Netayahu had bragged of the shining technological beacon that Israel was.

Now, Netanyahu's reputation was perhaps about to be shattered like the statue of a former ruler in Shelley's poem *Ozymandias*; where the broken monument to a one-time king of kings lay, half buried in desert sand, bearing the now empty threat:

"Look on my works, ye mighty, and despair!"

The remains looked out only on the wasteland around. No-one is there to hear – or fear. The empty threat of Ozymandias, was as empty as the lie that Mohammad, back in Nabi Saleh, had lost a portion of his head to a bicycle accident. The generals might continue shouting their lies, but in time less and less people would be listening. President Trump might agree with the Israeli government and generals, but he will be gone in time too.

I took my seat on the plane back to Stockholm. It was orderly and quiet. The uneventfulness contrasted with an exchange which had caught my ear on a flight into Tel Aviv a few days earlier, when a passenger had demanded that a steward get him a pillow.

"I'm sorry sir, we don't have any." The young steward replied politely.

"In that case get me the pilot's!" asserted the passenger, straight faced, and loud enough to get an audience.

If it was a joke, nobody laughed, and the young steward squirmed a little, and seemed less assured than he had a minute before, not sure what to say, or even where to look. A small incident, but some distance from the decorum which usually helps tens of people fit into a relatively little cylinder of air-bound metal. Of course, all nationalities have rude people. But Bassem had got me thinking about the mentality of the occupier with its *looking down the nose at others* approach.

How would Israelis and Palestinians live as neighbours in peace? I suggest that walking into your neighbour's garden, fully armed, after shooting a bullet into the head of their young cousin is far from the way forward. When the daughter of the house reacts angrily to this incursion and delivers a justifiable and understandable slap to the intruding soldier she ought not face months or longer in prison (even before trial) if peace is to be achieved.

On the plane back to Sweden I had to complete preparations for a lecture for a course in Technical English, to be delivered the next evening. I read an inspiring report about a small river in Wales, saved from acid rain and restored back to life. I would meet once again my students – young and optimistic, focusing on making the world better, through more effective use of energy and resources.

Around half of the student engineers in the class would be young women, some could be international visitors. Without much strain on my imagination, I could place Nour in amongst such a class in my mind's eye. In a few years Ahed and Marah could be amongst them, a few years after that Janna. Indeed, a few more years after that and Janna could be delivering the lecture! Instead they were struggling against a military Occupation. If not *in* prison, they might be waking in the night with the raids, or preparing, as in Nour's case, for court appearances and having to find huge amounts of cash for bail, and lawyer's fees.

These times were difficult for the young women, the girls and the mothers I had met in Palestine. Difficult too for the fathers, Bassem, Bilal and Fadel, and their sons too.

But the time was most difficult for those I had not been able to meet. Ahed, and her mother Nariman, and her cousins, Mohammad and Osama… and the many other political prisoners.

Fortunately, time passes through the most difficult of days, and in time this rotten Occupation will surely be defeated. Already, Ahed Tamimi is known by millions as a girl who *fought back* – a girl who fought back with *right* on her side.

Let us make sure she does not fight alone.

Notes

[1] http://mondoweiss.net/2017/12/should-israeli-journalist/.

[2] https://secure.avaaz.org/campaign/en/free_ahed.

[3] https://www.middleeastmonitor.com/20180213-un-slams-israel-for-violating-palestinian-teens-rights.

[4] http://www.palestinechronicle.com/great-concern-chile-calls-israel-release-ahed-tamimi.

[5] https://www.juancole.com/2018/02/letters-solidarity-tamimi.html.

[6] https://972mag.com/prominent-actors-musicians-and-authors-demand-ahed-tamimis-release/133119.

[7] http://mondoweiss.net/2018/01/israeli-apologizes-comparing.

[8] https://www.timesofisrael.com/military-court-indicts-soldier-slapping-teen-ahed-tamimi-her-mother.

[9] https://www.theguardian.com/world/2000/sep/29/israel.

[10] https://books.google.se/books?id=G820rBq299AC&pg=PA191&redir_esc=y#v=onepage&q&f=false.

[11] https://www.nytimes.com/1981/12/14/world/south-africa-needs-more-arms-israeli-says.html.

[12] http://www.independent.co.uk/news/world/middle-east/the-forgotten-massacre-8139930.html.

[13] http://www.nytimes.com/2003/02/13/world/sharon-faces-belgian-trial-after-term-ends.html.

[14] https://www.YouTube.com/watch?v=yV1HwG1_phs.

[15] https://www.nytimes.com/1995/01/25/world/a-wall-around-israel.html.

[16] https://www.un.org/press/en/2016/sc12657.doc.htm.

[17] https://www.haaretz.com/1.5105104.

[18] https://www.YouTube.com/watch?v=yV1HwG1_phs.

[19] *The Way to the Spring: Life and Death in Palestine*, Ben Ehrenrich. Granta Books 2017.

20 Ehrenreich, B. (2011). *Nickel and dimed : On (not) getting by in America* (1st Picador ed.). New York: Picador.

21 https://www.YouTube.com/watch?v=PauF73umk8k.

22 Interview with Bassem Tamimi, February 2018.

23 https://www.investigaction.net/en/nabi-saleh-is-where-i-lost-my-zionism.

24 https://www.theguardian.com/world/2014/feb/08/children-of-Occupation-growing-up-in-palestine.

25 https://www.haaretz.com/israel-news/.premium-israel-investigated-whether-ahed-tamimi-s-family-was-real-1.5762887.

26 https://www.facebook.com/search/str/haim+schwarczenberg/keywords_blended_posts?filters_rp_author=%7B%22name%22%3A%22author_friends_feed%22%2C%22args%22%3A%22%22%7D (post 25 Feb 2018).

27 https://www.haaretz.com/israel-news/tamimi-cousin-admits-wasn-t-shot-in-head-but-hurt-by-bike-crash-1.5850598.

CHAPTER 2

A Slap with Historical Roots

Ahed's slap in the face of the Israeli soldier was also an outcry of desperation over the humiliations, the massive violence, the forced evictions, the massacres, and the terror that millions of Palestinians have endured during the past seventy years.

14 May 2018, is the 70th anniversary of the founding of the state of Israel. It will be a day celebrated in Israel and among its supporters – all the way down to Donald Trump in the White House. But these celebrations will still offer only silence about the history which led to Israel's formation; for it was really written in blood, the blood of those who had lived on the stolen land.

Once the party is over, on 15 May, a much darker anniversary takes place. That day is commemorated by twelve million Palestinians as Yawm an-Nakba – the Day of the Catastrophe. The catastrophe, refers to the war unleashed upon the Palestinian people, when nearly a million were driven from their homeland in 1948. This day, and the consequences of what happened then, are inevitably lodged as a thorn in each and every Palestinian's heart, in Ahed's heart too. It is not the result of parents teaching their children to hate, as anti-Palestinian propaganda would have us believe. Instead, Palestinian children grow up with the consciousness that their parents, grandparents and great grandparents have lived through the same kind of injustice and terror as they face today. Military violence, forced expulsions, imprisonment, land theft, torture and murder are just as much part of a Palestinian family history as summer holidays, birthday parties, school exams, marriages, and the funeral of an old grandmother are part of any average Western World family's history.

A new perspective on *the slap* is gained with an understanding that it was a response to seven decades of this kind of suffering by Ahed's family, and her people, at the hands of the military machine. A machine, which on *that day* in December 2017 was represented by *that Israeli soldier* who trespassed into the Tamimi's garden.

It is not uncommon that people on the Israeli, as well as on the Arab, side claim that the conflict between Jews and Arabs, or Muslims, has existed "forever" and that it can never be solved. That "Muslims and Jews will never be able to live next to each other..." is a familiar assertion. It is also a falsehood. The conflict was not created by the Arab peasants who had been cultivating the land of Palestine for hundreds of years, nor by their Jewish neighbours, or the ordinary Jews who fled pogroms and racism in Europe. It was created by the imperialist ambitions of the ruling elites, who used religion and nationalism for their own interest. To prove it we need to take a look at the history of Palestine and how this conflict was created.

> "Ten years ago the Jews were living as Ottoman brothers loved by all the Ottoman races ... living in the same quarters, their children going to the same schools. The Zionists put an end to all that and prevented any intermingling with the indigenous population. They boycotted the Arabic language and the Arab merchants, and declared their intention of taking over the country from its inhabitants." [1]

This, from The Palestinian paper *Filastin* from 1914, making a clear distinction between Jews and Zionists. Under the old Ottoman Empire, Jews and Arabs had lived in peace, in Palestine.

In the 19th century most Jews and Arabs lived side by side in mixed communities. A Jewish quarter has existed for a very long time in Jerusalem but that is in no way unique for Palestine, such Jewish quarters or streets existed in many other Arabic as well as non-Arabic cities. But this was about to change, and the reason was not to be found within

Palestine. The seeds of conflict came from outside, from the imperialist Western powers.

Zionism has mainly expressed itself as the idea that the Jewish people have the right to, and should, form a separate nation-state. Zionism became a political tendency amongst Jews in Europe in the end of the 19th century. Ideas that every nationality should belong to their own nation-state were on the rise. But so too was anti-Semitism, and after outbreaks of large-scale pogroms in the Russian Empire in 1881-1882, the exodus of Jewish people from Europe started. A very small minority migrated to Palestine (about 35,000 by 1903, a tiny fraction of the two million Jews who had migrated to the USA by 1914).

In 1896, Theodor Herzl published the work *The Jewish State*[2] , which spoke about Palestine as "our unforgettable historic homeland." The first Zionist Congress was held in Basel in 1897, and founded the World Zionist Organization, whose goal was a publicly recognized home in Palestine, "for the Jewish people." By that time there were eighteen Jewish colonies in the country.[3]

This was the peak of European colonization of the world. The French conquered Algeria in the 1840s and took control of Tunisia in 1881. Together with Egypt, they built the Suez Canal which opened in 1869 and which, in 1875, became jointly controlled by France and Britain, who wanted to secure the sea and land routes to their most important colony, India. In 1882, the British military occupied Egypt, and Kuwait became a British protectorate in 1899. Explorers suspected that there could be big oil reserves in the region and the first big oil field was found in Persia (Iran) in 1908, which increased the interest of Western imperialism for the region. Morocco fell under French control in 1912.

During the First World War, Britain, in exchange for promises of Arabian independence, won over Arab leader Sharif Hussein Bin Ali and his son Faisal, who in 1916 led an uprising against Ottoman-Turkey and entered the war on the British side. What the British didn't tell the Arab leaders was that they, with the secret Sykes-Picot agreement of the same year, had agreed to divide up the Middle East between Britain, France and Russia. Following the Russian Revolution, the Bolshevik government led by Lenin and Trotsky, in a move to put an end to secret diplomacy and shady deals behind the backs of the people, made the Sykes-Picot agreement *public* in December 1917. After defeating the Ottomans together with the British, Hussein and Feisal started to realise that they had been double-crossed. At the UN conference in San Remo of April 1920, the Western powers agreed that Syria and Lebanon would be under French control and that the British would have the right to control Iraq, Jordan and Palestine. Faisal was driven out of Syria, by the French army, in the summer of 1920.

Against this background, Zionism, and the idea of Jewish colonization of Palestine, suited Britain, in particular, very well indeed. The revolutionary overthrow of the Russian Tsar in February 1917 sent shockwaves through the leading circles of Britain and France. Would Russia continue fighting on their side? The British government calculated that the sympathy of Russian Jews could be won through a pronouncement in favour of Zionism, which they hoped would keep Russia in the war. Another reason was that the British feared that the French, who had ambitions to take control over Syria and Lebanon (as they did in 1920), was also looking at Palestine. The Russians had strengthened their influence over the Black Sea and the eastern parts of the collapsing Turkish-Ottoman Empire. By appealing to religious heritage, and supporting the Zionists, the British hoped to also gain support from the US, where the biggest Jewish community, outside Europe, now resided. The ruling circles of Britain came to realize how they could use Zionism as a tool to keep Palestine under British control, and the British government became increasingly benevolent towards the leading British proponent of Zionism, Chaim Weizmann.

The British foreign secretary Arthur Balfour on 2 November 1917, declared that

"His Majesty's government views with favour the establishment in Palestine of a national home for the Jewish people, and will use their best endeavours to facilitate the achievement of this object."[4]

The strongest opposition to the Balfour Declaration actually came from the Jewish community itself. Jewish representatives in Britain protested against claiming special rights for Jews at the expense of the Arab population in Palestine but also, like the British Secretary of State for India, Edwin Montagu, himself Jewish, they expressed fear that the Zionist plans would worsen the situation of Jews in Europe and labelled the declaration: "Anti-Semitism".[5] In fact, Zionists remained a very small minority amongst Jews for some time to come. David Fromkin calculates that, in 1913, the last date for which there were figures, only about one percent of the world's Jews had signified their adherence to Zionism.[6]

The Zionists understood that they needed British protection since Jews were still a small minority in Palestine, less than 8% in 1914. A Zionist publication in London wrote:

> "'Democracy' in America far too often means majority rule … if this idea would be practiced in Palestine, what would happen then? … Qualitatively it's a simple fact that the Jews have the upper hand in Palestine and under the right conditions they will be dominant also quantitatively in one generation or two."[7]

The "right conditions" meant British oppression to prevent the Arabic majority from executing their democratic and national rights. The Palestinian leader Sharif Hussein tried in vain to appeal to the League of Nations, referring to the charter on the right to national self-determination, on which Balfour himself commented in parliament 1918:

> "…in Palestine we do not propose even to go through the form of consulting the wishes of the present inhabitants of the coun-

try …. so far as Palestine is concerned, the Powers have made no statement of fact which is not admittedly wrong, and no declaration of policy which, at least in the letter, they have not always intended to violate".[8]

The most important tool of the Zionist-led colonization of Palestine was the Jewish National Fund (JNF), which focused on buying up Palestinian land and distributing it to Jewish settlers. Previously, when land shifted owners in Palestine, the poor peasants working and living on the land, were allowed to stay. Now, they were forcefully evicted. In 1907, the writer, Yitzhak Epstein, described how she witnessed the purchase of the lands of Ras al-Zawiya and al-Metulla (in Hebrew Rosh Pina and Metullah) from absentee landlords and saw the subsequent anger of the dispossessed farmers: "The lament of Arab women … still rings in my ears. As they [left the land] they stopped to kiss the stones and the earth."[9]

The opposition against the Zionist project was growing. In 1910, the Haifa-based newspaper al-Karmil published translated extracts from Herzl's The Jewish State and some resolutions of the 1911 Zionist Congress. The editor of al-Karmil pointed out that the goal of the Zionists was to take over Palestine and urged Arabs not to sell land to them. At the 1913 Zionist Congress Arthur Ruppin complained that Jews in Jaffa were less willing to display "national solidarity" because they lived in mixed neighbourhoods with Arabs. By 1918, some 15,000 Jews were living in 45 rural colonies that made up the new Zionist camp – quite distinct from the 50,000-strong "old", non-Zionist Jewish community.[10]

In May 1920, Britain was granted the Mandate for Palestine by the newly formed League of Nations. The British Mandate ruled Palestine with the World Zionist Organisation as a de facto partner. At the same time, a Palestinian national identity was growing, partly in response to Zionism. In the beginning of the 1920's the opposition amongst Arabic people against Jewish colonialism was regularly bursting out in riots and violent confrontations. However, the Jewish trade union movement Histadrut, in December 1920, formed a volunteer defence organization called the Haganah (defence), which was to become the army of the forming Jewish state.

Hitler's rise to power in Germany, in 1933, accelerated the migration of Jews out of Europe, and 1935 saw the biggest influx of Jewish immigrants in one single year since the beginning of the Mandate – 65,000.

The opposition to Jewish colonization increased. Large demonstrations were held in Tel Aviv on 13 October 1933, and two weeks later, in Jaffa, British police opened fire on a crowd, killing 26 Arabs and injuring nearly 200. Protests followed in Nablus, Haifa and Gaza. The Arab population demanded a national government for Palestine, a halt to both Jewish immigration and land sales.

The Arab protests culminated in April 1936 with a general strike, civil disobedience and refusal to pay taxes – events that today are still called by Palestinians the "great rebellion", (al-thawra al-kubra). The movement quickly evolved into a civil-war-like situation. Crops at Jewish farms were burnt, trees were chopped down, and grenades were thrown at Jewish vehicles. Bombs exploded in Haifa and Jaffa, and the railway line to Egypt was sabotaged. By June 1936, the British high commissioner described "a state of incipient revolution."[11] In August 1936, the Lebanese guerrilla leader Fawzi al-Qawuqji arrived with a five-hundred-strong Arabic force, in an attempt to form a Palestinian army.

In October 1937, protests erupted all over the country, on an even wider scale than the previous year. Armed groups were formed, and buses, railways and the Iraqi oil pipeline were attacked. In the summer of 1938, rebels were in control of mountainous areas and patrolled openly in the streets of Nablus, the centre of the struggle. The number of rebels was estimated at 9–10,000. For five days the British army lost control over the Old City of Jerusalem.[12]

When the British colonialists later crushed the Arabian revolt, in 1938–1939, they, at the same time, taught the Zionist leaders everything they needed to know about how to terrorize a population. 25,000 British policemen and soldiers were sent to Palestine, the biggest force stationed outside Britain since the First World War. This was more than the total number of British troops in India. The brutal methods which drove the Nakba, the war, and subsequent exodus in 1948, were first used ten years earlier, by the British. These methods included punitive missions in villages, blowing up houses and uprooting crops. The regular practices of the Nakba – of attacking a village before dawn, using hooded informers to pick out rebels who were then put into metal wire cages, all had been modelled by the British military earlier.

The number of Jews serving in the police force grew from 3,000 in 1936, to 22,000 in 1939, the majority of which effectively served in the Haganah. The British officer Charles Wingate played an important role in transforming the Haganah into a professional military force, teaching them about military techniques and repression. Amatzia Cohen, who participated in these attacks claimed his force was instructed by a British sergeant in how to attack defenceless villagers, and that the sergeant had complained, "…you don't even have the basic knowledge in how to use the bayonet against dirty Arabs…".[13]

At the end of the uprising, about 5,000 Palestinians had been killed. The Palestinian leader al-Hajj Amin al-Husayni was expelled to Cairo in 1937. In putting down the uprising of 1936–1939, British imperialism prepared the way for the terror of 1947–1949.

David Ben-Gurion, who became the first prime minister of Israel, spelled out in a letter, from 1937, what the Zionist leadership was planning for:

> "We must expel the Arabs and take their places and if we have to use force, to guarantee our own right to settle in those places then we have force at our disposal"[14]

The same year, he added "...the reality on the ground [Arab majority] will make force necessary."[15] A key role was played by Josef Weitz, the head of the settler activity, with a remit to evict Palestinian families from land bought by Jews. Under Weitz the JNF prepared for large-scale evictions of Palestinian land, by making a detailed inventory of all Arabic villages, with specifics on roads, water sources, names of local leaders, political affiliations etc. At the start of the 1940s, Weitz wrote that taking over all Palestinian land was a "holy duty", and that:

> "Among ourselves it should be clear that in this country there isn't room for both peoples together. With the Arabs we won't achieve our aim of being an independent nation in this small country. The only solution is Palestine, at least a West Palestine [ie. The entire area west of the Jordan, as distinct from an 'Eastern Palestine' which refers to Transjordan] without Arabs...and there's no other way but to transfer the Arabs from here to the neighbouring countries, to transfer all of them. Not a single village, not one tribe should be left behind..."[16]

Members of the Haganah conducted reconnaissance tours in the villages to make plans of how to attack them.

In the 1940s, the Zionists felt confident enough to start attacking the British forces in Palestine, to push them out. Terrorist activity by the extreme Zionist groups Irgun and Lehi intensified. On 6 November 1944, the highest British representative in the Middle East, Lord Moyne was murdered outside his home in Kairo. In August 1945, the World Zionist Organisation called for open opposition against British rule in Palestine and, in October, revolt broke out. Railway lines were blown up in 153 places, and a wave of terror attacks against British installations in Palestine commenced. Even the British Embassy in Rome was bombed. In July 1946, The King David Hotel in Jerusalem was destroyed, in terror bombing, approved by the Haganah. Ninety-one people were killed. The attacks culminated in the blowing up of the British headquarters, in January 1947. Just one month later, the British had had enough, and announced that they would end the mandate and withdraw from Palestine.

Meanwhile, Zionism increasingly gained US support. A decision was taken in, April 1946, to admit 100,000 Jewish refugees into Palestine, following demands from US President, Harry Truman. Restrictions on land sales to Jews were removed too.

In April 1947, the British United Nations (UN) ambassador demanded that the status of Palestine should be up for negotiation in the General Assembly in the autumn. A UN Special Committee on Palestine (UNSCOP) was formed. In November 1947, the UN General Assembly adopted Resolution 181 on the Partitioning of Palestine, which would take place at the end of the British Mandate on 14 May 1948. The Jewish population constituted about 30% of the population and owned 5.8% of the land, but according to the UN plan, they would be given 55% of the land of Palestine.[17]

The official Israeli history of events in 1948, described as a Jewish *David's* fight against the Arabian *Goliath*, has little in common with actual facts.

In reality, the Palestinians were sacrificed not only by the Great powers who controlled the U N, but also by their Arab neighbours. Twelve days before the partition plan was adopted by the UN, King Abdullah of Jordan stuck a secret deal with the Zionists not to confront them, and accepted the forming of a Jewish state, in exchange for Jordan taking control over the West Bank. Britain, who was losing influence, gave their support to the secret deal. They tried to counterbalance the growing US influence by switching allegiances to the Jordanian regime. The British foreign secretary Ernest Bevin declared, "...the carrying through of this agreement depends on the British officers of the [Arab] Legion. That is why we shouldn't withdraw them from Palestine." Britain had no serious intention to confront the Haganah.

What now followed had been carefully planned since 1946, when David Ben-Gurion put forward the plan of what to do with Palestine's Arab population when the British left. "Plan C", as it was termed, (Gimel in Hebrew) and Plan D (Dalet in Hebrew) were prepared and included:[18]

- Striking at the Palestinian leadership.

- Striking at the Palestinian instigators and those who support them financially.

- Striking higher Palestinian officers and civil servants in the mandate administration.

- Hurt Palestinian transport.

- Hurt the sources of Palestinian livelihood: water sources, factories etc.

- Attack Palestinian clubs, coffeehouses, meeting spots etc.

On 2 November 1947, Ben-Gurion said that the Palestinians, "...can either be arrested *en-masse* or expelled; it's better to expel them." [19]

The morning after the UN resolution in November 1947, the 75,000 Palestinians in Haifa were targeted by the extreme-right paramilitary group Irgun, together with the Haganah. From their settlements on the hillside, the Jewish population started shooting at the Palestinian communities below, with rifles and grenades. Jewish soldiers rolled barrels filled with explosives and big steel bullets down into the Palestinian neighbourhoods. They also poured oil mixed with petrol in the streets and set fire to it. When terrified Palestinians came out from their homes, to put out the fires, they were sprayed with machine gun fire from the Jewish areas. Haifa had been an area with a strong working-class solidarity between the two communities. This is one reason why Irgun targeted Haifa and especially the oil refinery – to stir up antagonism and violence between the Arab and the Jewish workers there.

In this, the Zionist armed forces were quite successful. When Irgun threw grenades at a crowd of about one hundred Arab day-labourers, gathered outside the main gate of the then British-owned Haifa Oil Refinery to look for work, chaos broke out. Arab refinery workers and others attacked the Jewish refinery workers, resulting in dozens of deaths before the British army and Palestine Police units were able to take control. But the Zionists were not satisfied. Shortly afterward, Haganah entered the adjacent villages of Balad al Sheikh and Hawassa, where many of the refinery's workers lived, with the orders to "kill as many adult males as possible." The attackers fired into windows with their guns, torched the houses, pulled people out, and shot them point-blank. The Haganah report, available in Israeli archives, put the number of Palestinian Arab deaths at "about 70".

In Haifa the Red Cross concluded that the Haganah must have poisoned the water since an unprecedented epidemic of typhus suddenly erupted in the city, and claimed at least 70 deaths.[20]

The Zionist wave of atrocities spread throughout the country, with the obvious aim of driving the Palestinians from their homes and lands. On 12 December 1947, the Irgun killed 13 people in an attack against the Palestinian village al-Tira near Haifa. 20 more were killed in a terror bombing at the Damascus Gate in Jerusalem. The next day, 16 Palestinian Arabs were killed and 67 wounded in bombings in Jerusalem and Jaffa. The town of Jaffa also had a hundred of its homes set ablaze, by Irgun.

Ten people were killed by a bomb placed by Irgun in the Noga Cinema in Jaffa on 16 December. Two days later the Haganah carried out the so-called al-Khisas massacre in the Palestinian village which bore that name. The Haganah soldiers started randomly blowing up houses in the middle of the night while the villagers were asleep. According to the Haganah report, they killed twelve people; seven men, one woman, and four children. All of these atrocities are well-documented and undisputed. At the following meeting with the

"Defence committee" everyone seemed very pleased with the operation. The representative of the orthodox Jews said, "...we were told that the army had the ability to destroy a whole village and all its villagers – so let us actually do it!"[21]

This violence, and the partition plan, led to repeated spontaneous reactions among the Palestinian Arabs. Riots broke out in Jerusalem, claiming the lives of eight Jewish inhabitants. But the Palestinians lacked a strong leadership and organization. The British repression in 1936-1939 had deprived them of this. The Zionists had conducted thorough intelligence with a network of informers in the villages and were completely aware of how weak the Palestinian side was. Richard Crossman a British Labour MP commented that:

> "The Jewish Agency ... is really a state within a state with its own budget, secret cabinet, army, and above all, intelligence service."[22]

Spontaneous Arab violence as a reaction to the massacres was used by the Zionist leadership as an excuse to start the ethnic cleansing. On 15 February 1948, Qisarya along the coast was attacked and in only a few hours the whole village was emptied together with four additional villages the same day. The British troops in the police-stations stood by watching the events. At the same time Sa'sa was attacked and the Zionist commander Moshe Kalman recalled that:

> "...as a third of the village was blasted into the air. We left 35 demolished houses and 60 and 80 dead bodies when we were done (quite a few of which were children."[23]

Ben-Gurion commented, "A small reaction doesn't impress anyone ... Destroy a town district and you start to make an impression!" He recommended the meeting to... "continue terrorizing the countryside ... so that the passivity that has been reported ... remains."[24]

This was to be followed on 10 March 1948 with Plan D (Dalet): to systematically purge Palestine of Arabs: "These actions can be done in two ways: either through destroying villages (setting them on fire, bomb them and then mine them) ... in case of resistance the armed forces must be destroyed and the population must be driven outside of the country's borders."[25]

Ben-Gurion stated that it wasn't necessary to separate the "innocent" from the "guilty" and that it was time to cause "collateral damage": "Every attack must end with occupation, destruction and a purge."[26] The Haganah deputy chief of staff Yigael Yadin proposed that the word "retaliation" was abandoned for a more offensive approach, to instil a mood of aggression into the soldiers.

Complaints came from several representatives of local Jewish communities, in a number of areas, who tried to maintain good relations with their Palestinian neighbours. But these voices were isolated and unorganised.

As plan D began, on 9 April, Zionist forces occupied the village of Deir Yassin, west of Jerusalem. The Jewish soldiers entered the village, spraying the houses with machine guns and killing many. The remaining villagers were herded together and murdered in cold blood. Some of the women were raped and then killed. Fahim Zaydan was twelve years old at the time and saw his own family being killed in front of him:

> "... they called for my brother Mohammad and shot him in front of us. My mother started crying and while she crouched down over him – carrying my little sister Hudra who she was still breastfeeding – they shot her too."[27]

Zaydan was also shot but survived his injuries. 254 villagers were killed.

The Zionists made great use of the massacre in Deir Yassin. News about it spread like wildfire all across Palestine, causing tens of thousands to leave their homes in panic and flee across the borders. Little did they know then, that they would never be allowed back to their homes again.

In Haifa, British Major-General Hugh Stockwell informed the Jewish authorities, on 18 April, that he would withdraw the British forces, who had acted as a defence wall between the two communities. The Jewish commander gave the order: "...kill every Arab you encounter".[28]

In the early hours of 22 April, masses of terrified Palestinians filled the harbour area to try to find boats to take them away. The officers of the Jewish forces ordered their men to place 3-inch cannon on the hillsides above the harbour marketplace. From there they started shooting grenades at the Palestinians, causing panic. Masses flooded on to boats, peopled got trampled to death and boats got overfilled and sank. The scenes were so horrifying that General Stockwell received heavy criticism from the British government.

The Western Arab part of Jerusalem had been attacked by artillery since the beginning of January 1948. The British forces had disarmed the Palestinians, promising that they would protect them. In April, the Haganah entered Western Jerusalem and their head of intelligence reported that, when the district of Qatamon was cleansed, "...looting and destruction began. Both soldiers and citizens participated. They broke into the houses and took furniture, clothes, electrical equipment and food." Eight Palestinian neighbourhoods and 39 villages in greater Jerusalem were ethnically cleansed.

By April 1948, a quarter of a million Palestinians had been driven out and 200 villages destroyed.

The news of the massacres also spread into the neighbouring countries, and the Arab leaders came under pressure to act, following huge popular protests. On 15 May 1948, they declared war on Israel and allowed thousands of volunteers to go to Palestine to fight. Much has been made of this in Israeli propaganda, but the Arab forces suffered from a lack of organization and inadequate equipment.

Historians put the effective number of Arab combatants at a mere 25,000.[29] The self-defence forces of the Palestinian Arab villages numbered approximately 7,000 men, under arms. These forces were enormously outweighed by the Israeli army of 50,000 soldiers, half of which had been trained by the British army. Moreover, by the end of the summer of 1948 the Israeli ranks had swelled to 80,000. The Jewish forces were also able to circumvent the British arms embargo thanks to the Israeli Stalinist Communist Party which organized imports of weaponry from Czechoslovakia and the Soviet Union. By giving the Zionists support, the Soviet Union opportunistically hoped to gain influence. This was to little avail as the influence of the United States increased. France was also a major supplier of arms.

The Arab volunteers were unable to prevent the entire Palestinian population of 50,000 from being driven out of Jaffa in May 1948. People were literally driven out into the sea when Jewish soldiers shot above their heads while they were trying to clamber aboard hopelessly small fishing boats. Around Haifa, fifteen villages was uprooted and their entire population driven away. "Our army is marching forward, conquers Arabian villages, and their population is fleeing like mice"[30], Josef Weitz wrote.

After having rejected a proposal for surrender, the Palestinian village of Tantura was attacked by Israeli forces on the night of 22 May. The villagers were forced down to the beach. The women and children were driven away. The men were told to sit close together on the beach. An Israeli officer, Shimson Amshvitz, picked out small groups of men who were taken away and shot nearby. After the slaughter had stopped, two Palestinians were ordered to help dig mass-graves. In 1999, a man (of Jewish origin) who owned the tractors used, recalled that they buried 230 bodies.[31]

There were generally two Israeli military orders during the summer of 1948, either – "cleanse" the village of Arabs and leave the houses, or "destroy" the village entirely. That summer too, aircraft were used more systematically against the Palestinians. Saffuriyya was one of the first villages to be bombed from the air. The UN negotiated two shorter ceasefires in July 1948, but the Israeli attacks continued. Between the first and the second ceasefire, from 8-18 July, their forces uprooted and drove out 70-100,000 people.

The Swedish Red Cross Chief, Folke Bernadotte, who during the summer had tried to negotiate a ceasefire (as the UN mediator in the conflict) and demanded the right for refugees to return home, was killed by the notorious Lehi Stern Gang in September 1948.[32]

The atrocities continued. On 28 October 1948, the village of Dawaymeh, five kilometres west of Hebron, was attacked by Israeli troops who had been ordered to empty the place in one hour. The soldiers jumped out of their vehicles and indiscriminately started shooting people. The mukhtar (Village elder leader), Hassan Mahmoud Ihdeib, counted 455 people as missing, including 170 women and children. Afterwards, Israeli soldiers testified that people were burnt alive, women were raped, and children were beaten to death.[33]

In February 1949, a ceasefire was agreed between Israel and Egypt, and in April, with Jordan too. About 730 000 Palestinians had become refugees. In total, 531 villages, eleven city districts and small towns were destroyed.[34] The catastrophe was a fact – the Nakba, the war, had led to a mass exodus.

Jordan, who had no interest in self-determination for the Palestinians, occupied the West Bank. The UN General Assembly, in December 1948, passed Resolution 194, which made the return of the refugees a *prerequisite* for a peace agreement. Despite ignoring the rights of the refugees Israel was awarded the status of a full UN member in 1949.

In the 1950's there were regular skirmishes with neighbouring countries and Israeli forces frequently conducted "punitive" military operations across the borders. They motivated their actions by pointing to Arab intrusion – "infiltration" -on Israeli land. But 90% of all Palestinian "infiltrations" were socio-economical: Palestinians trying to return to their homes, sometimes to resettle, sometimes to get some of their belongings, or to try to harvest crops. During the period 1949 to 1956 alone, between 2,700 and 4,000 "infiltrators" were killed by Israeli forces, most of them unarmed.[35]

Backed by British and French forces, Israel invaded Egypt in October 1956, to try and overthrow the Egyptian president, Gamal Abdel Nasser, who with his left-leaning, pan-Arabic ideas was a strong contender against Western domination, and who, that summer, had nationalized the Suez-canal. The invasion failed after mass resistance in Egypt, and after US opposition too.

The occupation by Israel of the Sinai Peninsula in 1956 was secretly planned two years in advance, together with France. The French repaid Israel by helping them build a nuclear reactor at Dimona, which established the Israeli military nuclear programme. South Africa supplied Israel with uranium from 1965 onwards. Despite Israeli denials, the whistle-blower technician, Mordechai Vanunu, exposed the Israeli nuclear weapons programme in 1986, and there is little doubt that Israel has got nuclear weapons. Israel has continuously refused to sign the Non-Proliferation Treaty.[36]

In the 1950's a new generation took up the struggle in Palestine, inspired by the revolutions in China and Cuba, the radical pan-Arabism of Nasser, the overthrow of the monarchy in Iraq in 1958, the struggle in Algeria which won its independence in 1962, and the leftist Baath-party coming to power in Syria in 1963. Fatah was formed in the latter part of 1950's by a group of activists around Yasser Arafat. In 1965, Fatah started to conduct bomb-attacks and sabotage operations against Israeli targets. To try and keep control over the Palestinian movement the Arab states set up the Palestine Liberation Organisation (PLO) in 1964. Fatah was incorporated into the PLO which became an umbrella organization for several groups, such as the more radical Popular Front for the Liberation of Palestine (PFLP) and Democratic

Front for the Liberation of Palestine (DFLP) who were influenced by the Soviet Union.

A revolutionary wave swept Jordan in the latter part of the 1960's. King Hussein was nearly overthrown by mass protests in 1966. After years of rising tensions, Israel in June 1967, launched a sudden military attack against its poor neighbours Egypt, Syria and Jordan, as well as invading the West Bank and Gaza. In the so-called Six-Day War, the modern Israeli Army and Air Force completely obliterated the military of the three Arab states. As a result, the Syrian Golan Heights, the Egyptian Sinai Peninsula, and all that remained of Palestine – the Gaza Strip and the West Bank – came under Israeli occupation and Israeli military law.

The Israelis demolished villages in the West Bank and another 300,000 Palestinian refugees were created – most of whom fled to Jordan. Just as Israeli law has prevented the Palestinian refugees of 1948 from returning to their homes, Israel also barred the return of the Palestinians who fled in 1967.

The conquest of these territories was followed by the expansion of Israel. A new phenomenon saw the light of day: Settlements. Although repeatedly condemned as a violation of International Law, Israeli citizens, almost exclusively of Jewish ethnicity, began to migrate to the recently conquered parts of Palestine and Syria to build settlements on land belonging to the original inhabitants. This was often carried out by confiscating land by military order, after which a government-funded settlement could be created. A significant amount of the settlers were then, as they are often today, new Jewish immigrants from outside Israel.

The hostile attitude of the settlers, the theft of Palestinian land, the cutting down of olive trees, the setting fire to homes, the theft and even poisoning of water resources, has brought a nightmare existence to many Palestinians. Ahed has seen all of this in her lifetime; her village of Nabi Saleh had its spring (and much more) taken by the nearby settlement of Halamish. Unprovoked settler violence against Palestinians, aimed at driving them off their land, is one of the main problems for the inhabitants of the West Bank. The number of assaults by settlers on Palestinians rose from 168 in 2009, to 312 in 201, and 411 in 2011.

Nabi Saleh is far from the only Palestinian village or town subject to settler violence. Just a fortnight before Ahed was arrested, people from the Esh Kodesh settlement came to 48-year old Mahmoud Odeh's farmland, shot and killed him. This was immediately followed by an attack by settlers and Israeli soldiers against Odeh's village, Qusra, just twenty kilometres from Nabi Saleh. They injured several of the villagers, including a three-year-old child. This was just one of 180 settler attacks against Qusra in the past six years alone. This violence includes the killing of Mahmoud Odeh's nephew and the kidnapping and torture of a teenager from the village by settlers. These events are rarely covered in Western media.

The settler attacks are often carried out with impunity, and receive the support from certain higher echelons of Israeli society. Israel is a religious state, where religious laws can be used to govern much of the lives and attitudes of the people. Religious leaders have defended the uprooting of Palestinian olive trees, and when an eleven-year-old Palestinian girl was killed by settlers, Israeli religious leaders were reported to have justified the act, declaring that such a child will grow up to become an enemy.

Settlers can even use cars to kill or mutilate Palestinians. The *Palestine Chronicle* reports that:

> "Incidents involving Israeli settlers hitting Palestinians in the occupied Palestinian territory are a relatively regular occurrence, and are usually treated by Israeli security forces as accidents, even in cases when witnesses claim the car-rammings were deliberate." [37]

In August 2017, an Israeli settler vehicle struck, and killed, an eight-year old Palestinian girl in Nablus.

When Israel invaded the West Bank, the bulk of the Palestinian resistance moved into Jordan. Fatah and PLO set up its headquarters in the town of Karameh, bordering the West Bank, and broke loose from Arab government control.

When the Israeli Army attacked Karameh in March 1968 it back-fired, partly because the Fatah resistance caused the Israeli forces unusually high casualties, partly because Jordan now broke with its servile policy and intervened on the side of PLO, and also because it led to condemnations of Israel throughout the world.

As a result, the prestige of Fatah increased enormously and it attracted an influx of volunteers. Following the attack, there were nearly 20,000 pro-Palestinian Arab fighters in Jordan. Yasser Arafat became known throughout the world, and was elected as the chairman of the PLO in 1969.

The period of 1967 to 1970 was the high tide of Fatah and the leftists of the PFLP and DFLP. The position of the Jordanian monarchy was so weak that there was a situation of dual power inside the country. The Fatah-led opposition organized their own administration and in some instances collected taxes from the local population. King Hussain tried to limit the Palestinian influence, first in June 1970, by attacking PFLP-run refugee camps. This resulted in hundreds of deaths. After four aeroplane hijackings by PFLP in September, the King finally attacked the Palestinians with air bombing and tanks, in what was to be known as "Black September." Syria briefly intervened, crossing into Jordan, but retreated after threats from Israel and the US. Jordanian forces continued to push back Palestinian influence. By 1971, Yasser Arafat and the PLO moved their bases to Lebanon.[38]

The so-called Yom Kippur War in 1973, when Egypt and Syria attempted to take back what they had lost six years earlier, resulted in a peace accord between Egypt and Israel. Sinai was returned to Egypt, which then turned its back on the Palestinian cause.

In 1982, Israel launched a massive invasion of Lebanon to smash the PLO. The operation was planned by Defence Minister, Ariel Sharon, who also planned to install a puppet government in Lebanon led by the Christian Phalangist Party. After Yasser Arafat and the PLO leadership, and many of the PLO fighters had left Beirut, the Phalangists, on 16 September, were let into the Palestinian refugee camps of Sabra and Shatila. With the IDF standing guard outside of the camp, ensuring nobody left, the Phalangists were let loose. It is well documented that they committed unspeakable atrocities; raping, mutilating and murdering thousands of people. As the writer Robert Fisk noted in an article from *The Independent*:

> "The Israeli army sent the killers into the camps and then watched – and did nothing – while the atrocity took place. A certain Israeli Lieutenant Avi Grabowsky gave the most telling evidence of this. The Kahan Commission held the then defence minister Ariel Sharon personally responsible, since he sent the ruthless anti-Palestinian Phalangists into the camps to "flush out terrorists" – 'terrorists' who turned out to be as non-existent as Iraq's weapons of mass destruction 21 years later." [39]

Robert Fisk in the same article records that:

> "Of course, those of us who entered the camps on the third and final day of the massacre – 18 September, 1982 – have our own memories. I recall the old man in pyjamas lying on his back on the main street with his innocent walking stick beside him, the two women and a baby shot next to a dead horse, the private house in which I sheltered from the killers with my colleague Loren Jenkins of *The Washington Post* – only to find a dead young woman lying in the courtyard beside us. Some of the

women had been raped before their killing. The armies of flies, the smell of decomposition. These things one remembers."[40]

The Israeli invasion finally forced Arafat and the PLO leadership to withdraw to Tunis, where they lost some of their direct influence over events in Palestine.

In December 1987, decades of discontent in the occupied areas exploded into an uprising that took many leaders, including those of the PLO, by surprise. This was the Intifada. It was a revolutionary mass movement, the biggest in Palestine since the 1930s. But unlike 1936 when the actions were mainly rural and organized around villages, the Intifada was a more general movement led by an urban proletariat, first and foremost by the youth. The first Intifada also saw a leading role by women in the grassroots of the movement.

The preceding years had been a period of Palestinians organizing into student unions, trade unions and other associations, organizations which now channelled the protests in many ways. The Intifada was a movement of mass-disobedience; strikes, demonstrations, boycotts, refusal to pay taxes, youth and children throwing rocks at the IDF. The movement was largely coordinated by the Unified National Leadership (UNL) who kept the movement informed through pamphlets, leaflets, and radio broadcasts. From 1987 to the end of 1993, nearly two thousand Palestinians and nearly three hundred Israelis were killed. 120,000 Palestinians were arrested at some point during the uprising, and 120,000 Palestinians were injured.[41]

This led to the so-called Oslo Accords, which was based on the idea of a two-state solution to the issue – that is a nation state of Israel, and one of Palestine. The Israeli leaders were coerced by the US into opening a dialogue with the PLO. Already in 1988, the Palestinian National Council had stated that it accepted a two-state solution based on the 1947 UN partition resolution, and Yasser Arafat publicly recognized Israel in December 1988.

In September 1993 Israeli Prime Minister Yitzhak Rabin and Yasser Arafat agreed on a joint Declaration of Principles. The agreement promised self-rule regarding everything but security, initially in Gaza and Jericho, and later in the West Bank. The West Bank and Gaza would be treated as one interlinked territory. The occupied territories were divided into three zones:

> Zone A: Under total Palestinian National Authority (PA) rule; the Gaza Strip and 4% of the area of the West Bank including Jenin, Nablus, Ramallah and Bethlehem.
> Zone B: Under PA rule but with IDF in charge of security, 25% of the West Bank.
> Zone C: Under total Israeli control, 71% of the West Bank.

The Oslo Accords meant that eventually the whole of the West Bank, except for Jewish colonies, and military installations would fall under PA control. The agreement was celebrated as a victory of the Intifada. In 1996, Arafat was elected the first president of the PA with 88% of the vote and Fatah had the support of about two thirds of the electorate. The same year, support for "violent methods" was down from 57% to 8% amongst Palestinians, 67% were in favour of the "peace process".[42] But there were critics from the start, pointing to the fact that the accords did not offer any solution for the millions of Palestinian refugees, and that it didn't clearly state that Palestinians would get their own independent state, with clearly defined borders.[43]

On the Israeli side, 51% were in favour of a Palestinian state, but the Israeli right frantically and fanatically opposed the deal. In November 1995, Yitzhak Rabin was assassinated by a Jewish extreme-right fundamentalist, and, in 1996, Likud's Benyamin Netanyahu won the election. Netanyahu was openly opposed to the Oslo peace process and did what he could to sabotage it. Instead of building new settlements Israel simply expanded the existing ones. The settlement population increased from 115,700 in 1993 to 199,000 at the end of 2000 (excluding East Jerusalem).[44] Between the end of 1994 and November 2000, 740 Palestinian houses were demolished by the Israeli Army in the West Bank and the Gaza Strip (excluding East Jerusalem).[45] The negotiations finally collapsed in 2001, with the election of Ariel Sharon.

Ariel Sharon came to embody Israel's *turning away* from the peace process. Sharon's "walk" on the Mosque square in the Old City of Jerusalem in September 2000, together with more than 1,000 security troops, provoked the Second Intifada. After being elected prime minister in 2001 he led Israel onto a path of escalating violence, launching Operation *Defensive Shield* in 2002 – the largest Israeli military operation in the West Bank since 1967 – which killed 1,539 Palestinians and 441 Israelis.[46] The Israeli Defence Forces (IDF) broke their way through the Palestinian presidential compound, and put Yasser Arafat under house arrest. Sharon also started building the wall in the West Bank in 2003. This was accompanied by demands from Israel and the US, under George Bush, of a "new leadership" of the PA – in a way, to try to blame Arafat for the collapse of the peace talks – and Fatah responded by having Mahmoud Abbas elected prime minister. Arafat subsequently died, in 2005, under suspicious circumstances (very high levels of radio-active polonium in his body[47]) and Abbas was elected new president of the PA. In the same year, Sharon launched the Disengagement Plan, dismantling all Israeli settlements and withdrawing the IDF from the Gaza strip, only to make Gaza "the world's biggest prison" with tight Israeli control of all entrances, seaports, airspace and all passage of people and goods.

The new Israeli Prime Minister Ehud Olmert continued the disastrous and violent policies of Sharon with Operation *Cast Lead* – also known as the Gaza massacre – in which, from December 2008, to January 2009, around 1,400 Palestinians were killed. Olmert eventually ended up in jail in 2009 convicted of fraud, money laundering etc, which highlights the level of corruption in the leading political circles of Israel. Benjamin Netanyahu continued with more of the same. Operation *Protective Edge*, in 2014, wrought the worst bloodshed in the history of the Gaza Strip as between 2,125 and 2,310 Palestinians were killed (including approximately 550 babies and children).[48] An estimated 20,000 tons of explosives were used, when almost two million residents were bombarded day and night, for more than fifty days in the summer of 2014. In the 2015 election Netanyahu appealed even more directly to the extreme settlers' movement. On the surface the Israeli state is more dominated by extremists, more nationalist and chauvinist than ever. But this reactionary mood is based on fear and a lack of alternative. It can very quickly evaporate. The occupation is unsustainable in the long run, and the truth is that Israeli society has reached an impasse.

Ahed, and her family, have opened the eyes of millions around the world to the absurdity of the Israeli occupation. The brutality of Israel, as an occupying force, is an expression of its own ill health. But the situation for the Palestinians is intolerable:

- Up to as much as one third of all the stateless people in the world are Palestinians – around 5 million.[49] Out of the total number of 12.4 million Palestinians in the world, 5.6 were registered as refugees in 2015 by the UN (43 percent). 29 percent of them live in refugee camps in Jordan, Syria, Lebanon, the West Bank and the Gaza Strip.

- In 2017, the UN's Economic and Social Commission for Western Asia (ESCWA) concluded that Israel was an apartheid state.[50] This report was subsequently withdrawn after intense pressure from Israel and the US. But it remains firmly established that Israel enforces a dual legal system in the occupied territories; civil courts for the settlers – on the basis of being Jewish, whether they are Israeli citizens or not – and military courts for Palestinians, with a conviction rate of 99.74%.[51]

- The Gaza Strip is in a situation of acute humanitarian crisis, with a lack of basic necessities such as electricity and clean water. Over 1 million people are at risk of contracting waterborne diseases.[52]

At the same time, deep divisions are growing within Israeli society itself. Today, 21 percent of Israelis live below the poverty line, more than in Mexico, Turkey and Chile. Men, on average, earn 22 percent more than women, the fourth largest gender gap in the world.[53] After Operation *Protective Edge*, in 2014, the Israeli President, Reuven Rivling, expressed his worries over the mood in the Israeli society: "Immediately, with the silence of the cannons, and with a surprising speed, the public debate went back to terms like inflation, and the cost of living … it's already been for three years that the Israeli public is showing it's not satisfied with the current system." In previous generations Israel could be perceived as promising a better future for ordinary Jewish people fleeing oppression in other parts of the world. But the neo-liberal policy of public sector cuts, downsizing etc. has left neither Palestinians, nor ordinary Jewish people with any high hopes of a better future. In 2001 – the year of the Arab spring – the biggest mass protest movement in the history of Israel erupted. 430,000 people demonstrated under the slogan: "The people demand social justice", with the support of 90% of the population.[54]

Netanyahu portrays himself as strong and impossible to defeat. Donald Trump's recognition of Jerusalem as the capital of Israel on 6 December, 2017, seemed to confirm the image of an undefeatable Israel with the full support of the world's strongest superpower. In this regard we shouldn't forget that the Obama administration in 2016 increased US support to Israel to $3.8 billion per year.[55] But all the US money in the world can't save the Israeli rulers from the gradual undermining of a firm popular support. Netanyahu is again accused of corruption this year, 2018. This is nothing new. In his first term at the end of the 90's Netanyahu was accused of fraud, and again in 2000. Expensive cigars, jewellery, pink champagne, gigantic budgets for catering and for ice-cream (!), work done on his private home… The extent to which the Netanyahu family have had the state, and bribes, pay for a luxurious lifestyle is staggering. At the time of writing it's an open question if

Netanyahu will be able to survive in the face of the growing pile of scandals. The jailing of Ehud Olmert shows that this is not an isolated phenomenon. In 2012, Netanyahu´s foreign minister resigned after an indictment for fraud. The political effect of corruption for the few, combined with worsening living conditions for many, can explode in the face of the Israeli ruling class.

The protest movement in East Jerusalem in the summer of 2017 shows the limits of the Israeli state in face of mass protests. In July, the Netanyahu government decided to install new checkpoints with metal detectors and security cameras at the entrances of the Noble Sanctuary/Temple mount. This area is not only used for prayer, but also as a park and an urban centre with schools and public buildings, and the measures would have restricted the movement of Palestinians even further. This led to protest demonstrations of about 10,000 people. Despite attacks from Israeli police with horses, water cannons, rubber bullets, stun grenades, and even though several youths were killed, the protestors kept coming back. Within two weeks the Israeli state backed down and made a u-turn regarding the new checkpoints. A resident of East Jersusalem wrote on the internet: "The street has gone beyond all existing leaders and raised its voice." The Palestinian people, with international solidarity, and with support from those in Israeli society suffering from worsening conditions – those who are beginning to see through the Zionist lies, could stop the Israeli war machine with mass action. They could break the siege on Gaza and the apartheid regime in the West Bank, break the segregation and discrimination. As a part of a new Arab spring in the whole region the Palestinian people could finally take their destiny in their own hands. By supporting Ahed Tamimi and supporting the Palestinian struggle you can help this become a reality.

Notes

1. Ian Black, Enemies and Neighbours: Arabs and Jews in Palestine and Israel, 1917–2017 – p. Penguin UK (2017).
2. Theodor Herzl, *The Jewish State* – Penguin Classics; UK ed. edition (2010).
3. Ian Black, Enemies and Neighbours: Arabs and Jews in Palestine and Israel, 1917–2017 –p. Penguin UK (2017).
4. see http://avalon.law.yale.edu/20th_century/balfour.asp.
5. https://en.wikipedia.org/wiki/Edwin_Samuel_Montagu.
6. Fromkin, D, *A Peace to End All Peace: Creating the Modern Middle East, 1914–1922*, Penguin, London, 1991, p. 294.
7. Ingmar Karlsson, Roten Till Det Onda – Uppdelningen av Mellanöstern 1916–2016.
8. http://www.balfourproject.org/balfour-and-palestine/.
9. Ahmad H. Sa'di, Lila Abu-Lughod edit, *Nakba: Palestine, 1948, and the Claims of Memory* – pp. 289-290 (Columbia University Press, 2007).
10. Ian Black, Enemies and Neighbours: Arabs and Jews in Palestine and Israel, 1917–2017 – p. Penguin UK (2017).
11. Ian Black, *Enemies and Neighbours*, quoting the British high commissioner Sir Arthur Wauchope https://en.wikipedia.org/wiki/1936%E2%80%931939_Arab_revolt_in_Palestine.
12. Ian Black, Enemies and Neighbours: Arabs and Jews in Palestine and Israel, 1917–2017 – p. Penguin UK (2017).
13. Ilan Pappe, *The Ethnic Cleansing of Palestine*, p. 40.
14. William James Martin, *Ben Gurion: "We Must Expel the Arabs and Take Their Place"* – Counterpunch magazine, 11th March 2005.
15. Ilan Pappe, *The Ethnic Cleansing of Palestine*, p. 75.
16. Moshé Machover, *Israelis and Palestinians: Conflict and Resolution* – pp. 204 Haymarket Books (2012).
17. Ian Black, Enemies and Neighbours: Arabs and Jews in Palestine and Israel, 1917–2017 – p. Penguin UK (2017).
18. *Whalid Khalidi – Plan Dalet: Master Plan for the conquest of Palestine* – see – http://www.is-studies.org/authors/wkhalidi/Dalet-Master-Plan-for-the-Conquest-of-Palestine-Khalidi.pdf particularly useful are the appendix in this document showing the details of plan C and plan D.
19. Irene L Genzier – *Dying to Forget: Oil, Power, Palestine, and the Foundations of U.S. Policy in the Middle East*, p. 75 Columbia University Press (2015).

20 http://www.marxist.com/israel-biological-weapons1948.html Salman Abu-Sitta, Israels Dark History Revealed.

21 Ilan Pappe, *The Ethnic Cleansing of Palestine*, p. 85.

22 Quoted from: Ian Black, *Enemies and Neighbours: Arabs and Jews in Palestine and Israel, 1917–2017* – p. Penguin UK (2017).

23 Tim Wallace-Murphy, *The Genesis of a Tragedy: A Brief History of the Palestinian People* – p. 70 – Grave Distractions Publications (2016).

24 Ilan Pappe, *The Ethnic Cleansing of Palestine*, p. 107, 108.

25 Ilan Pappe, *The Ethnic Cleansing of Palestine*, p. 111.

26 Ilan Pappe, *The Ethnic Cleansing of Palestine*, p. 92.

27 Ilan Pappe, *The Ethnic Cleansing of Palestine*, p. 131.

28 Tim Wallace Murphy *ibid* p. 72.

29 Ingmar Karlsson, *Roten Till Det Onda – Uppdelningen av Mellanöstern 1916–2016.*

30 Ilan Pappe, *The Ethnic Cleansing of Palestine*, p. 131.

31 Ilan Pappe, *The Ethnic Cleansing of Palestine*, p. 170.

32 http://www.independent.co.uk/news/world/middle-east/israels-forgotten-hero-the-assassination-of-count-bernadotte-and-the-death-of-peace-934094.html.

33 See https://unispal.un.org/DPA/DPR/unispal.nsf/0/2DBED30E8FC680878 5256D600063E9C4.

34 Avi Shlaim – *Israel and the Palestinian – reprisals, revisions and reputations* p. 58 Verso (2010).

35 https://en.wikipedia.org/wiki/Palestinian_political_violence.

36 Jonathan Cook – *Why Israel is still afraid of Morchechai Vanunu* – Electronic Intifada – 28th June 2004 https://electronicintifada.net/content/why-israel-still-afraid-mordechai-vanunu/5134.

37 See here palestinechronicle.com/8-year-old-palestinian-girl-dies-after-being-struck-by-israeli-settler-car-in-nablus/).

38 For some further insight into these incidents see an Al Jazeera report from 20th July 2009, here: https://www.aljazeera.com/programmes/plohistoryofrevolution/2009/07/200971385345398771.html.

39 Robert Fisk, *The Forgotten Massacre,* The Independent Friday 14th September 2015 http://www.independent.co.uk/news/world/middle-east/the-forgotten-massacre-8139930.html.

40 Robert Fisk ibid The Independent 14th September 2015- also see video report here – https://www.youtube.com/watch?v=-pWwkVfbY10.

41 https://en.wikipedia.org/wiki/First_Intifada.

[42] Per Garthon, Palestinas Frihetskamp p. 376, p. 384.

[43] http://www.lrb.co.uk/v15/n20/edward-said/the-morning-after.

[44] http://www.pij.org/details.php?id=269.

[45] https://www.btselem.org.

[46] https://en.wikipedia.org/wiki/Operation_Defensive_Shield.
https://www.un.org/press/en/2002/SG2077.doc.htm.
https://www.btselem.org/download/200207_defensive_shield_eng.pdf.

[47] https://www.theguardian.com/world/2013/nov/06/yasser-arafat-poisoned-polonium-tests-scientists.

[48] https://en.wikipedia.org/wiki/2014_Israel%E2%80%93Gaza_conflict.
https://www.btselem.org/index.php/press_releases/20160720_fatalities_in_gaza_conflict_2014.

[49] https://www.statelessness.eu/blog/world%E2%80%99s-stateless-new-report-why-size-does-and-doesn%E2%80%99t-matter.

[50] https://www.middleeastmonitor.com/wp-content/uploads/downloads/201703_UN_ESCWA-israeli-practices-palestinian-people-apartheid-occupation-english.pdf.

[51] https://www.middleeastmonitor.com/20160610-49-facts-about-israels-occupation-of-the-west-bank-and-gaza-strip/.

[52] http://www.who.int/emergencies/response-plans/2018/occupied-palestinian-territory/en/.

[53] https://www.israelnationalnews.com/News/News.aspx/206392.

[54] https://www.theguardian.com/world/2011/sep/04/israel-protests-social-justice.

[55] https://www.reuters.com/article/us-usa-israel-statement/u-s-israel-sign-38-billion-military-aid-package-idUSKCN11K2CI.

Timeline

1550–1400 BCE	Independent Canaanite city-states under the supremacy of the Egyptian Kingdom.
1020 BCE	Hebrew kingdom under King David.* Before and during this period Philistines and other people also live in Palestine and there are intermarriages and joint celebrations of religious feasts etc.
740 BCE	The region becomes part of the Assyrian empire.
550 BCE	The Persian King Cyrus conquers the area after a short period of Babylonian rule during which Jews are being deported. Jews are allowed back to settle side by side with other people, tribes and nationalities.
330 BCE	Alexander the Great conquers the coastal strip of Palestine.
63–132 BCE	After several wars and changes of rulers the area integrates into the Roman Empire.
326	The emperor Constantine makes the byzantine Palestine a centre of Christianity.
636	Palestine is conquered by the Islamic Empire.
1099–1187	The Christian crusaders controls Jerusalem and most of Palestine before it is taken back into Muslim control by Egyptian sultan Saladin in 1187.
1516	The Ottoman Turks conquer Palestine and rule for four centuries.
1840	Britain intervenes on the side of the Ottomans against Muhammad Ali of Egypt.
1840's	France conquers Algeria.
1869	The Suez Canal opens, built by France together with Egypt.
1875	France and Britain control the Suez canal.
1880's	France occupies Tunisia in 1881 and Britain occupies Egypt in 1882.
1882	The first wave of Jewish emigration from Europe, most go to the USA, a small number start to build settlements in Palestine. In 1878, 15,000 Jewish people live in Palestine. In 1914, 59,000 or 7.4% of the population.
1896	Theodor Herzl publishes "The Jewish State" which speaks about Palestine as "our unforgettable historic homeland".
1897	First Zionist Congress in Basel. World Zionist Organization is founded.
1916	Sharif Hussein Bin Ali joins Britain to defeat the Ottoman Empire, without knowledge of the secret Sykes-Picot agreement between Britain, France and Russia. Hussein and his son Feisal are driven out of Syria in 1920.

* The historicity of this is questioned. There is little evidence outside of the Bible of a United Kingdom of Judah and Israel in the 10th century BCE, and no direct evidence concerning King David.

1917	The Balfour Declaration announces Britain's commitment to creating a Jewish "national home" in Palestine.
1920	Britain is granted a "mandate" over Palestine by the League of Nations.
1936–1939	The Great Palestinian rebellion. Britain sends 25,000 troops to Palestine.
1945	First Jewish revolt against British rule in Palestine.
1947	29 November, United Nations adopts resolution 181 on the partitioning of Palestine and the ending of the British mandate.
1948	The Nakba. 14 May, The British mandate ends. Between 800,000 and 1 million Palestinians are expelled and made refugees. More than 1,000 Palestinians are killed and 531 villages destroyed. https://imeu.org/article/quick-facts-the-palestinian-nakba
1949	A ceasefire is agreed (although refugees are not allowed to return) and, despite breaking UN resolutions, Israel is recognized as a full UN member.
1956	Coronel Nasser nationalizes the Suez Canal. Israel, together with Britain and France, invade Egypt. The invasion backfires and strengthens Nasser's authority.
1959	Fatah is founded in Kuwait. Yasser Arafat becomes the movement's leader.
1962	Algeria wins independence from French rule.
1964	The Palestine Liberation Organization (PLO) is founded in January by 13 Arab nations to try and contain the Palestinian independence movement. PLO's "parliament", the Palestine National Council (PNC) convenes in May to elect an executive committee.
1965	Fatah launches its armed struggle against Israel.
1969	Yasser Arafat becomes the leader of PLO which has transformed to an umbrella group for Palestinian groups fighting for independence.
1967	Israel launches the 6 day war, invading the Gaza Strip and Sinai, East Jerusalem and the West Bank as well as the Golan Heights. Another 400,000 people become refugees. Israel starts to annex the West Bank through settlements.
1967–1970	A period of dual power inside Jordan where the Hashemite monarchy is challenged by Palestinian guerrilla groups who conduct several airplane hijackings and attacks on Israel. The influence of the PLO and Fatah is at its peak.
1970	"Black September" where the Hashemite monarchy launches a war against the Palestinian movement and forces them out of Jordan. The PLO leadership moves into Lebanon.

1973	The Yom Kippur War, Egypt and Syria attack Israel to retake the Sinai peninsula and the Golan Heights but is thrown back by the Israeli counterattack.
1977	The Likud government under Menahem Begin intensifies the building of settlements.
1978	The Camp David Accord leads to the return of the Sinai to Egypt. Egypt becomes the first Arab state to recognise Israel.
1982	Defence minister Ariel Sharon launches the invasion of Lebanon. Arafat and the PLO leadership are forced to withdraw from Beirut to Tunis. The Phalangists commit atrocities in the Palestinian refugee camps Sabra and Shatila killing 2,000–3,500 people.
1987	The Intifada, a movement of Palestinian mass resistance, breaks out in December. It lasts until 1991, and in a smaller form until 1993. 1,352 Palestinians and 100–160 Israelis are killed.
1991	The Madrid Conference in October leads to negotiations between Israel and PLO.
1993	In September Yitzhak Rabin and Yasser Arafat agree on a Joint Declaration of Principles, with the aim of Palestinian self-rule in Gaza and the West Bank.
1994	Yasser Arafat and the PLO leadership return to Palestine and establish themselves in the Gaza Strip.
1995	In November Yitzhak Rabin is killed by a religious Jewish extremist.
1996	Yasser Arafat is elected president of the Palestine National Authority (PA) with 88% of the vote. Benyamin Netanyahu of Likud is elected prime minister of Israel, and declares war on the peace process.
2000	Negotiations in Camp David between Yasser Arafat and Israeli prime minister Ehud Barak under the supervision of Bill Clinton fail to reach an agreement. Ariel Sharon conducts the "walk" on the mosque square in Jerusalem which provokes the Al-Aqsa (second) Intifada.
2001	Ehud Barak suspends the peace talks to try and appease Israeli critics and win the election, but loses to Ariel Sharon, who is elected new prime minister.
2002	As a part of "Operation Defensive Shield" Israeli army invades Ramallah and Arafat is put under house arrest.
2003	As a response to Israeli and US demands for a "new leadership" for the Palestinians, Mahmoud Abbas is elected prime minister. George Bush launches a "road map" for Palestine. Israel starts building the wall in the West bank.

2005	Arafat dies and Mahmoud Abbas is elected new president of the PA. Sharon launches the Disengagement Plan, dismantles all Israeli settlements and withdraws the IDF from the Gaza Strip. All entrances, seaports, airspace and all passage of people and goods is controlled by Israel, making Gaza "the world's biggest prison".
2006	Ariel Sharon declares his intentions to scrap the "road map". Hamas wins the parliamentary election of the PA which leads to a split between the PA led by Abbas in the West Bank and Hamas ruling the Gaza strip.
2008	In December Israel invades the Gaza Strip in Operation *Cast Lead* to stop Hamas' rocket fire into Israel. Between 1,166 and 1,417 Palestinians are killed and 13 Israelis. The conflict is ended in January 2009.
2011	Biggest social mass protests in the history of Israel. In September 430,000 demonstrate across Israel under the slogan "The People demand social justice".
2014	Israel invades the Gaza Strip in Operation *Protective Edge* – the worst bloodshed in the history of the Gaza Strip. 2,251 Palestinians are killed including 551 children.
2015	Benyamin Netanyahu is re-elected prime minister.
2017	Donald Trump announces that the US recognizes Jerusalem as the capital of Israel, leading to protests in several countries. Ahed Tamimi and her cousin Nour Tamimi are jailed for slapping an Israeli soldier intruding into their home. Ahed's mother Nariman is also jailed.
2018	Ahed is kept in custody, as is Nariman. Mohammed and Osama Tamimi (sons of author Manal) are held in prison. Nour is released on bail (5 Jan).
	A worldwide protest develops to get Ahed and her fellow Tamimi prisoners released.
	By the end of February almost 2 million have signed a petition to demand Ahed's release.
	Hundreds of child prisoners remain in Israeli military prisons.
	The Israeli police launch an investigation into corruption and Israeli PM Netanyahu.

By Peter Lahti.

CHAPTER 3

The Criminalising of Palestinian Children

The trip from East Jerusalem to Ramallah is not a tough one if the car works, and you know what to expect. If your GPS fails, as it did on the car journey I was on, it can make you tense. When the GPS works again, it is easy to doubt what it's telling you, especially when you travel from the pristine motorway around Jerusalem, and then hit the dusty roads as the check point to Ramallah approaches. Suddenly you are in a traffic jam near that checkpoint and it all becomes very real. Here is an Israeli military show of strength – rifles and barbed wire – and there is the wall, a partition of giant concrete slabs. On the wall, a drawing of Yasser Arafat, the former Palestinian leader – a giant work of graffiti, next to more huge protest art – a boy with a slingshot, casting a stone – standing up to the checkpoint, with the greeting "Welcome to Palestine" writ large.

One pot-holed road veers off to a refugee camp, the other to Ramallah. The tension increases when your travelling companion tries to do a u-turn when all traffic is bumper to bumper, not the best idea. The driver was the author of the previous chapter, Paul Morris. He had rang me a few weeks earlier about the idea of this book. Once through the checkpoint, the tension eases. You're on the way to the Ramallah city centre, and then hopefully onwards to Nabi Salah.

The viral video of Ahed standing up to the soldier and her subsequent to arrest and imprisonment, was the reason behind this book and this chapter. This chapter is about Ahed and the hundreds like her. Because sadly she is not alone. There are literally hundreds of children in Israeli military jails.

From Ramallah to Nabi Salah the drive is about 30 minutes. It helps that the man giving directions is the father of Ahed Tamimi –

he knows the way, his family can trace their roots to the area back for hundreds of years. We met Bassem Tamimi earlier in Ramallah. He is a proud and articulate man. An activist who along with his family, and the community of Nabi Salah have been protesting against illegal Israel occupation not just near his village, but across Palestine.

Arriving near the village you are struck by the immediacy of the Israeli settlement. There is no mistaking it. A large Israeli flag – the size of a billboard adorns the entrance. The fencing appears to be brand new, as does the very large gate. It is the Ikea of all settlements. Having just travelled for 30 minutes through the magnolia landscape of Palestine, and viewed some of the small enclaves, this settlement is not just illegal, but the way it is built tells you that the state of Israel is making a statement.

Another two minutes the village of Nabi Salah comes in sight. It is up a small hill. It is striking that at the bottom of the hill is a watchtower. Installed by the Israeli Defence Force (IDF), it reminds me of similar towers that I've seen in Newry and Crossmaglen in Northern Ireland installed by the British army. It is no doubt designed to keep a watch on the village and to add extra strategic pressure to the community as a whole. Palestine – we are watching you! There is also a gate at the bottom of the hill. This long metal gate is periodically locked by the IDF, making it difficult for people from the village to leave.

Shortly after Ahed was arrested, graffiti appeared in the village.[1] The graffiti spray painted at the entrance stated "There is no room in the Land of Israel for the Tamimi family." Other graffiti scrawled on walls proclaimed "regards from the retaliation unit of the Israel Defense Forces" and "a death sentence for Ahed Tamimi." Needless to say this had been painted over. There is little doubt that the nearby settlers, or maybe soldiers from the IDF had taken this action at the perceived humiliation to their armed forces.[2] The graffiti again is designed to intimidate, and isolate the village. It won't work.

On arriving in the village Bassem introduces us to Bilal and his wife, Manal. I had been in touch with Bilal a few days before by e-mail which I found through his *YouTube* page.[3] He wanted initially to meet earlier in Ramallah, but apologised as he had to attend a military tribunal for his son who was in detention, earlier that day. Needless to say his response humbled me – the fact that he had time to respond, and was keen to meet was a great opportunity – and here I was.

Bilal is quiet and modest. This belies a deep determination and radicalism. One sight of his *YouTube* page gives a clear idea of his boldness in recording the resistance to the occupation by the IDF. His filming has not only served to alert the world to the resistance in Nabi Saleh, but his film footage has been crucial in ensuring that activists who participate are exonerated from trumped up charges from the IDF.

Bilal introduces me to his wife. I had seen Manal from a video Bilal had e-mailed that had featured on *Al Jazeera*. In "How to be a Palestinian Supermom" Manal outlines the struggle against the IDF and also her part in that the resistance.[4] Bilal knows that I want to speak about the justice system in the Occupied Palestinian Territories (OPT), and so he is keen for me to speak with Manal.

Bilal and Manal Tamimi have four children. In many ways they are an ordinary family with the worries that all parents have for their children – are they eating healthy food, are they doing well at school, and will the children grow into good people? But in reality, they are not an ordinary family, the occupation has made them extraordinary.

The family has been at the forefront of the campaign of ongoing peaceful mass resistance against military occupation. Those heroic mobilisations of Palestinian workers and youth in villages have throughout the OPT been well documented.[5] It has also lead to Bilal and Manal being imprisoned on numerous occasions over the last decade. This represents a change in the struggle since the second *Intifada* – protests using the tactic of mass resistance has sprung up all over the West Bank. This has seen ordinary families, including children, taking the Palestinian resistance to the IDF on a town by town basis.

The IDF's violent and brutal response shows just how brave Ahed's aunt, Manal, has had to be. She has been shot by the Israeli military – not only with rubber coated steel bullets, that often happens, no, a live round in the left leg. As Manal casually reports:

> "The day I was shot it was the 12th April 2016 just one month after I was released from prison. I got a threat through twitter, it said 'Today your blood is going to be spread on the street.' It's a tweet, I thought it's not important. So I went down to the protest, and suddenly I hear a crash. I realise that it's my leg – I didn't understand what's going on, I thought it maybe a steel coated rubber bullet – so I hold my leg and start to jump to stay away from the soldiers. Then I realised I was shot with a live bullet via a sniper with a silencer, so they actually knew who I am. It was not a random shooting. Then I had tweets later saying – 'we nearly killed you,' and 'we wish you that you died." [6]

At the time of writing, their two sons, Mohammed and Osama, were being held in prison. Understandably, their welfare is their current and main concern. They are being detained by a military court system that is brutal, and increasingly, ordinary people are becoming more and more aware of this.

The military court system and military law in the OPT, according to the Israeli state, was to "…enable the existence of sound governance, security and public order." [7] The reality is, it is a vehicle for repression.

The military courts were established even before the end of the Six Day war. Military Proclamation No.3 "Concerning Security Provisions" outlined the jurisdiction of the military courts, its regulations and operational procedure. In 1970, these initial proclamations were replaced by Military Order 378, "Order Concerning Security Provisions" in the West Bank – with a similar one operational in Gaza. These orders expanded the scope and jurisdiction of the military courts over a whole range of "security charges" since 2005, the Military Court system only operates in the West Bank, where Order 378 continues as the primary piece of legislation.[8] Whilst the claim by the Israeli state claims these measures are merely intended to promote "sound governance" and are necessary to prosecute security related offences, the reality is somewhat different. The military legal system extends to deal with non-security related offences, even traffic offences. The reality is that this is a judicial system designed to repress Palestinians. Israeli settlers in the OPT are not dealt with under the same rules. It is a form of Apartheid, far from equality before the law. As a delegation of British lawyers noted in their report to Parliament:

> "Within Israel and the West Bank the two legal systems in operation are different. Israeli citizens (including the settler population in the West Bank) are subject to Israeli civilian and criminal law and the Palestinians in the West Bank are subject to Israeli Military Law."[9]

In effect, there is one rule for one person, and a completely separate rule for another. Manal explains it like this:

> "In the west Bank we are under military law. At the same time the Israeli settlers are under Israeli civilian law. So, for example, if there are two children, one Israeli and one Palestinian, throwing stones at each other, to the point where they get arrested, the Israeli child is taken to a police station and kept, to keep him out of trouble. Not as a prisoner. His parents are contacted and they collect him and take him home. But, the Palestinian child will be taken to an interrogation centre, interrogated, and sometimes tortured – shouted at! He will then be transferred to the prison, an adult prison, and worse than that, most of the Palestinian children, they are put with Israeli criminals, so you can imagine how bad that is. It is done to scare and intimidate."[10]

Article 64 of the Fourth Geneva Convention does permit an occupying power to establish military courts. However, in establishing them they must follow and adhere to certain standards – "...set up in accordance with the recognised principles governing the administration of justice."[11] It is stressed that they must not be used as an "...instrument of political or racial persecution"[12] It is clear that the Military Court system does not meet these standards, and a vehicle for political and racial persecution.

The status of the Military Court system is that it does not adhere to "recognised principles" governing the administration of justice. The Defendant should have the right to know what he is being charged with and in a language that he understands. Under Art.71 of the Fourth Geneva Convention and Article 14(3) of the International Covenant on Civil and Political Rights, it states that if charged with a crime the *defendant* is to be:

> "...informed promptly and in detail in a language which he understands of the nature and cause of the charge against him"[13]

This is not the reality in the OPT. For a Palestinian defendant it does not come close to a recognised legal standard. Often, and if the defendant is lucky, they may be made aware of the charges brought against them at the first hearing – this is after the charges have been filed with the Court prior to the first hearing. At that first hearing a Palestinian defendant is expected to respond immediately – nether the defendant or lawyer has had the opportunity to prepare a response, or study the evidence. Effectively they are bounced into making a plea there and then the military court system permits lengthy periods between hearings, and restricts families of the defendants from attending.[14]

Manal Tamimi considers the whole system as absurd.

> "It is not a court, it is a fake court, if you go to it for example they don't have a translator for the families and for the prisoner

himself. All of the time you find the translator on his phone, on Facebook or Twitter. The translator may translate two words out of 100 words, so by the end the family and the prisoner are lost and they don't know what the discussion is about – they don't know what are the charges, what is going on. The Judge most of the time is distracted."

In further breach to international judicial standards, there is no presumption of innocence. The military court system does not place a burden on the prosecution to prove guilt, the burden is effectively shifted to the defence. The independence and impartiality of the military courts has come into question.[15] This cannot be of too much of a surprise, as highlighted in the documentary *The Law in the Parts,*[16] all of the judges are sourced from the military itself.

The failure to follow legal norms has led to an unprecedented level of incarceration. Since the Israeli occupation of the Palestinian territory in 1967, more than 800,000 Palestinians have been detained under Israeli military order in the OPT.[17] As a sample – in 2006 only 0.29% of the nearly 10,000 cases concluded in a military court found a defendant not guilty.[18] Of those convicted approximately 95-97% are as a result of plea bargains – this indicates that Palestinian defendants and lawyers do not trust the system to deliver justice if they do opt for a full hearing.[19] For many Palestinians the process is lengthy and time consuming. Many defendants have been subjected to physical and/or psychological torture which result in "confessions" which are then used to secure to convictions and plea bargains.

Bilal, Manal and almost everyone in the village of Nabi Salah has direct experience of the military court system. Everyone I met had been in prison a number of times, and if not, an immediate relative had been. Their experiences confirm the reality of a system, that as a matter of international law, is deeply discriminatory and fails to follow legal norms. Manal explains it:

"The military court is a biased court. The Judge is not better than the interrogator, the interrogator is not better than the soldier who is torturing the prisoners – so all of them are part of the same system. There is no justice whatsoever, so you cannot say the Judge, he is neutral, he is not. The [defence] lawyer he should provide evidence that the prisoner is not guilty and the Attorney General, he should prove that this person is a criminal. It is not like that. It is always the Attorney General, the judge the whole system – everything is against the prisoner and the [defence] lawyer – so it's a specific court just to show the world that – 'ok there is democracy and justice in Israeli Courts, here we bring a Palestinian, there are hearings and sessions.' It is true there are [defence] lawyers but it is all about what the interrogator and the General Attorney wants. It is all about criminalising Palestinians – even when they are innocent, to find excuses, fake reasons most of the time and fake charges just to put them in prison."

The military court system exceeds its powers. Art. 64 of the Fourth Geneva Convention allows military courts to prosecute issues relating to security.[20] As a matter of international law the occupying power should respect local laws. This has been ignored by the Israeli state – the military court system now prosecutes on all matters unrelated to security questions – from unauthorised building to other minor offences, such as traffic offences – it exceeds its remit and its powers. This further enforces the state power of Israel over the local population. The real significance of the Military Court system is to re-enforce Israeli state domination over all aspects of Palestinian daily life and its institutions. As a matter of international law, if a military court system is established by an occupying power, then military courts should apply equally to all people in that territory. There is no evidence of Israeli citizens or settlers – who, having committed an offence in the

OPT are then tried in the military courts under military legislation. So, if a Palestinian and an Israeli settler commit identical offences they will be tried in a different court, with different procedures[21], and will inevitably result in different sentences.[22] A Palestinian is likely to face prison, or a heavy fine, an Israeli settler will not face the same severity. This is a system of apartheid.

The effects of military law are wide ranging and the jurisdiction of the military courts are broad. Thus, suppression of Palestinian political rights, cultural rights and forms of non-violent protest are prosecuted freely. The military court system is established to suppress dissent and victimise Palestinians for political activity. International law is supposed to prevent such racial persecution.

Speaking with Manal she explains the reality of political dissent, the consequences of the military court system and how it operates:

> "My first arrest was in January 2010. This was one month after we began our protests from the village. I was at the protest, but prior to then I was reluctant to get involved – I thought I am now a wife and mother. But I got involved because they [IDF] shot a gas canister inside the house normally we want to evacuate the children, but the soldiers tried to force us back inside the house. To take children back inside the house full of tear gas that is suicide, you are sending them to their death – so I refused. They arrested me and my sister. They interrogated us for nine days. Then they moved us from the interrogation centre to prison for Israeli criminal women, not Palestinian. All the time the Israeli women tried to attack us. Can you imagine two Palestinian women who wear a head scarf amongst 100 Israeli women who are in prison for criminal offences? All the time they tried to attack us. At one point they put is in a shared cell with 20 young offenders – they were drug offenders and drunk. We just hugged each other and stayed in the corner of the cell to avoid attacks."[23]

Gaby Lasky, lawyer for Ahed and for many of the young people from Nabi Saleh understandably is critical of the whole "justice" system

> "We have to remember that this is a military court, and it's a court of occupation…The real task of this court is not to enact justice, but to perpetuate occupation. There are two sets of rules in the occupied territories, depending on your nationality or ethnicity, while settlers will be brought to an Israeli civil court, Palestinians – for the same offense – will be brought to military court, where the rules are different, where it is much harder, where the punishments are harsher and where children are kept in detention for the end of the trial." [24]

Israel as the occupying power in the OPT has responsibilities under the Hague Conventions,[25] the Fourth Geneva Convention, and the Regulations annexed to them. Israel has accepted that the Hague Conventions are applicable , but they contest the applicability of the Convention.[26] The Israeli state argue that the West Bank and Gaza Strip were not sovereign territory – that is a state in and of itself – and thus Israel claims that its role in the OPT is that of "administrator" leaving it unaccountable under the Fourth Geneva Convention.[27] What Israel is essentially seeking to escape, amongst other issues is, that the Convention prohibits occupying powers moving people into territory they occupy.

The position of the state of Israel sets itself squarely against that of global consensus and they are wrong as a matter of international law. Since 1967, international legal community has confirmed that the state of Israel as the occupying power in the OPT cannot evade the obligations and commitments it gave (just like any country) as a party to the Geneva Conventions – it cannot pick and choose how international law applies. The United Nations Security Council (UNSC) and the General Assembly (UNGA) has repeated a position through resolutions and statements that the Fourth Geneva Convention applies to the OPT and

Israel cannot unilaterally absolve itself of this.[28] Indeed, in a further blow to their unilateral stance the International Court of Justice in its July 2004 *Advisory Opinion on the Legality of Israel's Annexation Wall in the West Bank* emphasised that "...civilians who find themselves in whatever way in the hands of the occupying power.." must remain protected persons[29] "...regardless of the changes to the status of the occupied territory as is shown by Article 47 of the Convention."[30]

It gets worse. In the area of international human rights law, the state of Israel has attempted to argue that human rights norms do not apply to the OPT.

As a matter of international of international human rights law the Universal Declaration of Human Rights (UDHR), the International Covenant on Civil and Political Rights (ICCPR) and the International Covenant on Economic, Social and Cultural Rights (ICESCR) reflect customary international law and are applicable to Israel in the absence of a binding treaty.[31] As a result they apply not just to Israel, but as a matter of legal function, to persons living under occupation.[32] Israel has accepted, in principle, all of the core UN international human rights, since 1967, but as an occupier, the Israeli government has rejected the applicability of human rights treaties to the OPT.[33] It neither makes legal sense, or even common sense, and has left them open to ridicule which they try to deflect with bombast and bluster.

The position taken by the state of Israel is rejected by the international legal community and the UN Human Rights Committee has repeatedly taken the position that the international human rights conventions apply to the OPT[34], and to all persons within it.

Given this, Israel is compelled to apply a number of Conventions relating to wider human rights to the OPT and the Palestinian people. These include the prevention of racial discrimination, the prevention of torture, the rights of the child and the protection of fundamental civil and political rights.

The Israeli state is in breach of not only international human rights law, but also international humanitarian law. It enforces a dual system and a discriminatory legal system. The Israeli state grants settlers the protections of Israeli civil law under the Israeli court system, at the same time Palestinians living in the same territory under military law have to undergo the military court system whose legal procedures violate international legal standards when administering justice. Flowing from this is a system that allows settlers from Israel in the OPT a freedom of movement, and protections under the law that Palestinians are simply denied. Palestinians are not only denied protection under international humanitarian law and human rights laws, they must seek justice through the military court system, which, as we have shown, is designed to effectively deny them exactly that.

In 2017, 15 Palestinian children died as a result of Israeli forces' actions, including a child who succumbed to injuries he sustained during an Israeli drone strike in the Gaza strip in 2014.[35] The United Nations Office for the Co-ordination of Humanitarian Affairs (OCHA) reported at least 961 child injuries at the hands of Israeli military in 2017.[36]

Ahed was arrested as a result of Israeli military aggression in Nabi Salah. On 15 December 2017 Mohammed Tamimi, 15, was shot in the face at close range with a rubber coated steel bullet. The rubber bullet lodged in the back of his skull and cause severe bleeding in his brain.[37]

Palestinian children in the West Bank, face arrest, prosecution, and imprisonment under an Israeli military detention system that denies them basic rights. Stemming from this Israel shamefully and systematically prosecutes between 500 and 700 children in military courts each year.[38] It is also of concern that ill-treatment in the Israeli military detention system remains "…widespread, systematic, and institutionalized throughout the process," according to the UN Children's Fund (UNICEF) report *Children in Israeli Military Detention Observations and Recommendations*.[39]

The simple statistics are damning: between 800 to 1000 children are detained every year; children as young as 12 can be prosecuted in military courts; approximately half of all detained children are arrested at night and report physical and psychological abuse during arrest, transfer and interrogation; over 99% of cases in the military courts end in conviction and approximately 50% of Palestinian child detainees are held in prisons in Israel in breach of Art.76 of the Fourth Geneva Convention – that is transferring them over a border.[40]

The United Nations Convention on the Rights of the Child (UNCRC), was ratified by Israel in 1991. The UNCRC was established to protect the rights of children and to acknowledge that they have a lower maturity and are more vulnerable than adults. The UNCRC seeks to build upon the principles of non-discrimination, the inherent right to life, and ultimately the best interests of the child. The preamble to the Declaration of the Rights of the Child notes that the child deserved protection by reason of physical and mental immaturity "… needs special safeguards and care including appropriate legal protection before as well as after birth" and that "The child shall enjoy special protection, and shall be given opportunities and facilities, by law and by other means, to enable him to develop physically, mentally, morally, spiritually and socially in a healthy and normal manner and in conditions of freedom and dignity. In the enactment of laws for this purpose, the best interests of the child shall be the paramount consideration".[41]

The relevant major provisions of the UNCRC are:

- Article 3: the best interests of the child are to be a primary consideration.

- Article 6: the right of every child to life and to development.

- Article 12: the right of the child to be heard, especially in judicial proceedings.

- Article 28: the right of a child to education.

- Article 37: the child's right not to be subjected to torture or to cruel, inhuman or degrading treatment or punishment; to arrest and detention being a measure of last resort and for the shortest appropriate period of time; to humane and dignified treatment in custody, including family contact; to prompt access to legal advice and representation; and to a prompt hearing before an independent court.

- Article 40: the state's duty to provide non-penal measures where appropriate and desirable; to treat accused or convicted children with dignity and with a view to rehabilitation; to accord the child full due process, including legal assistance and interpretation where appropriate; and not to require self-incrimination.

Israel is a full party meaning it should abide by the UNCRC. It has not proposed any reservations or made representations as to why it does not apply to the OPT.[42] Given that Article 2(1) of the Convention provides: "State Parties shall respect and ensure the rights set forth in the present Convention to each child within their jurisdiction without discrimination of any kind..."[43] – as a matter of law, the ICJ's Advisory Opinion, states that the UNCRC applies to the OPT. It stated at 113:

> "As regards the Convention on the Rights of the Child of 20 November 1989, that instrument contains an Article 2 according to which "States Parties shall respect and ensure the rights set forth in the ... Convention to each child within their jurisdiction ... That Convention is therefore applicable within the Occupied Palestinian Territory."[44]

There are a number of politicians who claim that the law as applied to Israel is unfair. They argue the basis of questioning the system of military law is to attack Israel itself and its existence. But this is again more bluster, and is a smokescreen. Israel is not the only country to have been challenged as to the applicability of international law as an occupying power.

It is in fact worth noting that the decision on applicability was held against the United Kingdom by the European Court of Human Rights as an occupying power in Iraq. In the case of *Al-Skeini v United Kingdom*[45] it was held that a state in military occupation has by virtue of it being a signatory to a human rights treaty – in this case the European Convention of Human Rights – has those extended in full to the occupied population who they have "physical power and control",of who inhabits an area of which the contracting state has effective control. The same principle, as a matter of international law, applies to Palestine and the Palestinian people. Israel is not a special case, and as a matter of law cannot have special treatment.

Day to day life for Palestinians revolves around Military Orders. On June 7, 1967, the day the Israeli military occupied the West Bank, Israeli authorities issued Military Proclamation No. 2. This order confirmed that the military commander would have full legislative, executive, and judicial powers over the West Bank.[46]

The authority to arrest and detain Palestinian children is found in Military Order 1651. Its scope is wide. It provides for a minimum age of criminal responsibility at 12 years and there is jurisdiction over any person 12 years and older. Children under the age of 12 cannot be prosecuted in the military courts, but Israeli forces will routinely detain children under 12 and question them for several hours before releasing them to their families or the PA.

Sentencing is also set out in Military Order 1651. For a child aged 12 to 13 they can be given a custodial sentence of six months. For a child of 14 to 15 the sentence can be up to 12 months, unless the offence carries a maximum potential sentence of five years of more.[47] Although the age of majority was raised to 18 years in September 2011, it still allows for 16 and 17 year olds to be sentenced as adults.[48]

As a result of the military legal framework, the Israeli army or police have the right to arrest even children without a warrant where they have a suspicion that the child has committed an act violating one of the "security offences". Most children are arrested on suspicion, without arrest warrants, and as *DCI Palestine* reports there is no independent review of how or why arrests have been made.[49]

Throwing stones is one of the biggest reasons for arresting a child, it is even a specific offence under Military Order 1651, which provides as follows:

- Throwing an object, including a stone, at a person or property, with the intent to harm the person or property, carries a maximum penalty of 10 years in prison.[50]

- Throwing an object, including a stone, at a moving vehicle, with the intent to harm it or the person traveling in it, carries a maximum penalty of 20 years in prison.[51]

In case the soldiers have a sensitive personality, incredibly, also under Military Order 1651, a child can also be arrested for insulting or offending a soldier's honour. This comes with a potential maximum penalty of one year in prison. Then the saving clause, any act or omission that "…entails harm, damage, disturbance or danger to the security of the region or the security of the [Israeli military], or to the operation, use or security of a road, dirt path, vehicle or any property of the State of Israel or of the [Israeli military]"[52] the maximum penalty for act or omission – is life in prison. It is equally shocking to note that any soldier or indeed police officer has the authority to arrest without a warrant where there is a suspicion that a Palestinian has committed an act which violates one of the offences in this broad category – this includes children. Accountability is minimal, independent oversight is non-existent – welcome to the OPT.

Palestinians in general, and children, in particular, when detained, face a totally oppressive Israeli state prison apparatus. It is a network of military bases, interrogation centres and detention centres spread across the West Bank and in Israel itself. Some of these facilities are based in the Jewish only settlements in the West Bank.

Palestinian children are held inside this network in order to be interrogated. Very few are released early and most are held in detention until the initial court appearance. After appearing in one of the military courts, child detainees are then moved to one of the prisons – many of these facilities are located inside Israel. Such a transfer is a breach of Article 76 of the Fourth Geneva Convention.[53] As stated, the settlements – which themselves are a breach of international law – are part of the military detention network establish by the state of Israel.[54]

As Manal Tamimi points out:

> "There is a strategy by them (the military) to arrest the youth, especially the minors, it is easy to terrify them and manipulate them, and so to incriminate them. So, when you have a 13-year-old in the interrogation centre with soldiers and without his parents, without a lawyer – which is a right to have a lawyer – they do not tell him his rights. Arresting minors is used, because maybe his parents are activists, so it is a message that if we are not able to break you, if you are not afraid of us putting you in jail, or shooting you or whatever, we will target your children – which is the worst thing for any parent."[55]

Since 2000, approximately 8500 Palestinian children have been detained, interrogated, prosecuted and imprisoned according to *DCI Palestine*.[56] Each year, it is estimated that 700 children (12-17 year olds) face arrest and prosecution. The military legal system is like a grotesque conveyor belt set to criminalise a generation.

The Convention on the Rights of the Child (CRC) prohibits torture and other cruel and degrading treatment or punishment. It provides that parties to the Convention must "…take all appropriate legislative, administrative, social and educational measures to protect the child from all forms of physical or mental violence, injury or abuse…"[57] The Committee on the Rights of the Child (UNCRC) has stated also that, "…disciplinary measures in violation of article 37 of CRC must be strictly forbidden, including corporal punishment, placement in a dark cell, closed or solitary confinement, or any other punishment that may compromise the physical or mental health or well-being of the child concerned."[58] Sadly this does not appear to deter the IDF or the military legal system. UNICEF, in February 2013, warned that the Israeli military detention system was to be condemned, as its treatment of children detainees suffer ill-treatment that is "…widespread, systematic and institutionalized throughout the process, from the moment of arrest until the child's prosecution and eventual conviction and sentencing."[59]

When UNICEF released an update on its report in February 2015 it noted that allegations of ill-treatment of children "…have not significantly decreased in 2013 and 2014."[60] Of the 38 UNICEF report recommendations, the UNICEF February 2015 update stated that "…four are in progress, 15 are partially addressed, 14 are under discussion, four are closed, and one has been rejected."[61] This is seemingly a work in progress with no sight to an end.

The treatment and arrest of Palestinians is a shameful. The treatment of children is scandalous. A number of reports illustrate that ill treatment begins from the moment the child is arrested.[62] Palestinian children are blindfolded and have their hands tied on arrest.[63] Three out of four experience some form of physical violence during arrest, prior to or during interrogation.[64] As is well documented by *DCI Palestine*:[65]

> "Recent amendments to Israeli military law concerning children have had little to no impact on their treatment during the first 24 to 48 hours after an arrest, where most of the ill-treatment occurs at the hands of Israeli soldiers, police, and interrogators."[66]

The UN Convention against Torture, as a matter of law, precludes the use of excessive force by police, military or other law enforcement agencies. It states that excessive force amounts to torture and ill treatment.[67] Given that hands are bound, often painfully with plastic[68], children are routinely blindfolded and taken from their homes, and frequently experience some form of physical assault on the way to the Israeli military vehicle – this amounts to torture.[69]

The way an arrest is conducted sets the tone. As reported in the UK Parliamentary report, *Children in Military Custody:*

> "Children, sometimes as young as 12 often at night are arrested, and have their hands tied using unlawful and painful methods, before being transported to an interrogation centre, sometimes on the floor of military vehicles. In the course of the arrest process, the vast majority of children interviewed have reported physical and verbal abuse. It is unclear whether they are told their rights at this stage or at all"[70]

In its report in 2013 the UNCRC reported its deep concerns with regard to the way in which the state of Israel was conducting itself in the arrest and treatment of Palestinian children. It condemned the Israeli army and the way in which Palestinian children are routinely treated and humiliated. It stated that the process was routine and they were tantamount to torture. The UNCRC has demanded an end to these violent acts and the ongoing targeting of Palestinian children.[71] As shocking as the thought of a 12-year-old child being arrested by armed forces is, it is reported that even children as young as 6 years of age have been arrested.[72]

In arresting Ahed at night, as described in the previous chapter, the IDF were carrying out what is a routine policy for them – many Palestinian children are frequently arrested at night.[73]

Once arrested, tied, and blindfolded many Palestinian children are subjected to further violence during the transport to the interrogation centre.[74] Recently *Military Court Watch* a charity based in the West Bank reported from 530 child testimonies collected between 2013-2017 that 64% had been subjected to physical violence.[75] The Israeli military argue that they carry out these arrests at night to limit disturbances. The reality is, the night time arrests are designed to intimidate, disorientate and according to *B'Tselem* in their report:

> "Palestinian teenagers from East Jerusalem are pulled out of bed in the middle of the night, unnecessarily handcuffed and then made to spend a long time waiting for their interrogation to begin. Only then, when they are tired and broken, are they taken in for lengthy interrogation sessions, without being given the opportunity to speak to a lawyer or their parents before the questioning begins and without understanding that they have the right to remain silent." [76]

Ahed is from a political family. They have been leaders in the strategy of mass resistance for many years. However, being arrested and being unprepared is a terrifying experience for anybody, let alone children. At the time of arrest it is possibly the last time a family will see their child again until they appear in court this could be several days, or even weeks later. As *DCI Palestine* record:

> "Night arrests traumatize children, distort feelings of personal security when at home and during sleep, and can hinder a child's ability to sleep in the future. Night arrests also have a significant impact on other family members, specifically parents who are helpless to protect their child and younger children that witness the violent arrest of their sibling." [77]

As a matter of international law, arrest and detention should only be used as a last resort. Therefore, there is no justification for night arrests. The UN Convention on the Rights of the Child states that "…in all actions concerning children […] the best interests of the child shall be a primary consideration." [78] The state of Israel, continues to arrest children at night. Promises made to the UN to phase them out appear to have been short lived. [79]

Children arrested at night are often then left, often tied and blindfolded until the morning.[80] They are given a cursory medical and often strip-searched.[81] During interrogation Palestinian children face threats from the armed forces to provide a statement, physical force is often used. If no statement is provided, additional threats are made to arrest other members of the family to further pressurise to confess or incriminate others. Gaby Lasky, Ahed's lawyer, expressed profound concern that Ahed had been threatened in this way. As mentioned, in the earlier chapter, she was told if she remained silent (which she has the right to do) that members of the wider family and would be arrested. That it is not idle threat can be inferred from the fact that mass arrests have indeed been carried out. One can also conclude from this Ahed has stood firm.

It is during this early interrogation that many children are not seen by a lawyer or a family member – this is by design. The right to silence is a fundamental right, (even more so for children, who should be considered even more vulnerable) – yet they are often not told of this right and denied access to a lawyer. As noted by *Lawyers for Palestinian Human Rights,* "The exclusion of a lawyer from a fundamental process in the investigation of a suspect provides unequal and unfettered power in the hands of the Israeli military."[82]

It is therefore no surprise that in a report by the NGO *No Legal Frontiers,* Palestinian children are often convicted by the Israeli military courts as a result of confessions.[83] As the UK Parliamentary delegation states:

> "According to Defence for Children International, 69% of children interviewed make confessions after a process that DCI describes as 'typically, a coercive interrogation' Defence for Children International reports that the physical and verbal abuse described above occurs not only during arrest and transportation, but also during interrogation. The children we spoke

to all reported that this treatment continued into the interrogation, where some were beaten until they confessed. Some also stated that they had reported this to the judge at their hearing, but said they had been ignored." [84]

No access to a lawyer, threats, abuse, and forced confessions. This is what faces Palestinian children when detained by the Israeli authorities. This is a situation that faces parents and activists throughout the OPT. Manal Tamimi tells me:

"...here in the village we began to make lectures for children about their rights in case they are arrested, the right of silence, the right to have their parents, the right to see a lawyer, how they should deal with the interrogator, deal with the soldiers in the way while they are transferring them. We also brought ex-prisoners to talk to the children about their experiences also..." [85]

For a child, the transfer between their home, to the interrogation centre, to the prison is on the metal floor of a military vehicle. This is as it was when Ahed was arrested. Soldiers are often sat around. Child detainees, again, as is the case with Ahed, are often taken into detention into Israel itself in breach of international law. When arriving at an interrogation or detention facility, a child is often kept in conditions which are designed to further intimidate. Manal Tamimi reports that she also prepared her children:

"We know they are going to arrest them [children], we prepare them for arrest since they were children, but it does not matter how much you prepare, for it is when you are in the experience that it matters. If I didn't educate Osama and Mohammed about what they should do in interrogation and how to deal with it, they won't be able to be strong enough to go through this experience so in the time that we are teaching them to learn or teaching them how to break the wall of fear inside them and how to control the fear, not letting the fear control them, how to stand for their rights. We teach them also to be human."

There are reasons for the IDF to isolate and disorientate children. As Manal has now found out from her son Mohammed, who was forced to watch his younger brother interrogated as a method of psychological abuse.

> "Also in the case of my children Osama and Mohammed, for example, while they are not minors but the way they dealt with them was equally bad. They let Osama watch his brother during the interrogation and forced him to watch so to break him. They said, tell us that you threw stones and we will stop torturing your brother"[86]

The worries of Palestinian parents, and the abuse their children face, is in stark contrast to what an Israeli child would face. For example, Israeli civilian juvenile justice system includes a number of protections for children in conflict with the law – including no interrogation at night, no arrest at night, and a parent present, but Israeli military law contains no comparable provisions.

Contrast that with the treatment of Palestinian children in the OPT who are repeatedly and systematically abused when interrogated.[87] A Palestinian child endures the use of restraints (usually plastic digging into their flesh), threats of, and actual physical violence. Additionally, there is a repeated failure to properly advise children of their rights, their right to see a lawyer, or family member. Indeed in 416 out of 429 cases (97%), children were denied access to legal counsel prior to and during interrogation, and did not have a family member present during questioning.[88] Threats and psychological torture are common, and faced with this onslaught, is it any wonder that they sign statements? Those same statements are presented to them in Hebrew, a language which is not generally understood by a Palestinian child.[89] To add insult to injury, routinely, child prisoners are denied water, food and access to toilet facilities.[90]

This is the situation that faces families and children up and down the OPT. For any parent it is a duty to prepare a child for life, but that preparation and that life should be for a new school, or a first love, or going to University. Preparing a child for inevitable arrest must be difficult.

The UNCRC expects that "...every child deprived of liberty shall be treated with humanity and respect for the inherent dignity of the human person, and in a manner which takes into account the needs of persons of his or her age."[91] There is an absolute prohibition on torture or other cruel, inhuman or degrading treatment or punishment. It is hard to see how the state of Israel is living up to any benchmark of international law or international standards when it comes to Palestinian children.

The military court system does not exist to administer justice. It is a practical tool of the occupation. It acts to legitimize control of the Palestinian population. Judges and prosecutors within the military court system, are active members of the Israeli military system. They are subordinate to military discipline and dependent on military superiors for promotion. Without doubt they are part of the system that continues to legitimise and enforce occupation. They are not independent or impartial.

Military prosecutors are usually legally qualified. However, some are still studying law or are in training. Military judges must have five years of legal experience and must hold the rank of captain. Palestinian defendants do have the right to an attorney but can be prevented from meeting their lawyer for up to 90 days.[92] Lawyers acting for defendants must be able to speak and read Hebrew as cases are conducted with Arabic translation. In administrative detention cases, lawyers for defendants often will not be provided with prosecution material due to the absence of interrogation notes and information is withheld for "security reasons."[93]

Depending upon the age, a Palestinian child must appear before a military court within 24 to 96 hours. Once in the courtroom, the child will often see a lawyer for the first time. However, this is the start of a lengthy process, and will involve multiple visits to court, journeys to and from prison, and waiting in the court, as the case is built against them, is routine. The system drags. The journey to and from the court can take an entire day, as often, and against international law, the child is held in Israel rather than in the OPT. The journey will leave a child exhausted emotionally and physically.

A Palestinian child will first appear in either Ofer or Salem military court. At court the Palestinian child will arrive shackled in their brown prison uniform. Until their case is called, they can wait for hours and often do not know when it will be called. Whilst parents are informed of the hearing dates, there is no certainty as to the time the case will be called – and so days can be wasted in court. Once the case is called there is no physical contact permitted with their child.

As a matter of international law a child should not have their liberty denied for long periods. The pre-trial detention, which is common in most cases, should only be if the child presents a serious risk of causing significant harm to others.[94] The UNCRC has stipulated that a final judgment should be delivered within six months – despite this, the majority of Palestinian children are held in pre-trial detention.[95]

The military justice system allows for a Palestinian child to be detained for up to a year before the possibility of legal proceedings being completed. At the time of writing, Ahed's trial has already been postponed so that she has been in detention over two months, at the time of writing. If not completed in this time frame, then the case will appear before an appeal tribunal and extensions of three months of a time can be granted.[96] Compare that treatment to an Israeli child. The civilian criminal juvenile justice system in Israel stipulates that a trial must begin within 30 days. Further, if the trial does not conclude within six months, the defendant must be released. A child under the civil code can be detained up to a maximum of six months and there is no remand for a child under 14.[97] An apartheid system for juvenile justice.

As we have seen, interrogation sessions serve as one of the main ways of gaining evidence against a Palestinian child. Intimidation and physical abuse is routine.[98] There is no independent oversight over how arrests are conducted. As a result abuse is inherent in the system. In addition, the Israeli military can arrest without warrants. They can arrest a Palestinian child on suspicion without evidence and detain. This further leaves the system open to abuse. As DCI Palestine notes –

> "A child's own confession or incriminating statements from other children are often the foundation of the Israeli military prosecutor's case against a child... [and yet] ... Military court judges tend to attribute a great deal of weight to defendant confessions and statements by arresting Israeli soldiers, according to DCIP attorneys."[99]

The fact that "confessions" are made without a lawyer fundamentally questions the veracity of the process. Despite this, incriminating statements and confessions are rarely excluded on these grounds.[100] As a result of the slow process, the false confessions, the waiting in detention, no chance of bail, the fight to obtain legal counsel inevitably pushes children to plead guilty:

> "Regardless of guilt or innocence, Palestinian children overwhelmingly plead guilty in return for a lighter sentence. The alternative would be a prolonged period of remand that would likely exceed any sentence imposed from a plea agreement, according to DCIP attorneys."[101]

Sentences for Palestinian children can be harsh. For a single charge of stone throwing, a child aged between 12 and 13 years can receive up to six months in prison. A child 14 and 15 years of age, can in law, receive the maximum penalty of 10 or 20 years. A 16 or 17year old has no child specific exemptions under military law and can receive the maximum sentence of 20 years – the same as an adult. Throwing a stone – a common offence – is dealt with under Military Order 1651.[102]

At the time of writing it is impossible to predict what the sentence for Ahed might be. One cannot rule out that a member of the Israeli elite demands that they see sense and realise that the longer Ahed is held the whole military court system, and the occupation is seen to look cruel and unjust – because Ahed has the sympathy of millions. However, such potential for reason has not stopped them holding Ahed for months, pre-trial, in a blatantly unjust way. It is entirely possible that Ahed's sentence is excruciatingly long.

Following recommendation from the UNICEF report, in 2013, Israel established youth courts under the military justice system. However, Manal Tamimi disputes that there is any real difference:

> "No, it's one system. It is against any Palestinian it doesn't matter if he is 7 years old or if he's 100 years old. So everybody goes through the same procedure, the same system…"

The report from the UK Parliamentary delegation concluded as follows:

> "…[there] are certain undisputed facts which compel us to conclude that Israel is in breach of articles 2 (discrimination), 3 (child's best interests), 37(b) (premature resort to detention), (c) (non-separation from adults) and (d) (prompt access to lawyers) and 40 (use of shackles) of the United Nations Convention on the Rights of the Child. If the manner of arrest and detention is to a significant extent that which is described in paragraphs 36 and 37, Israel will also be in breach of the prohibition on cruel, inhuman or degrading treatment in article 37(a) of the Convention. Transportation of child prisoners into Israel is in breach of

article 76 of the Fourth Geneva Convention. Failure to translate Military Order 1676 from Hebrew is a violation of article 65 of the Fourth Geneva Convention." [103]

Military Court Watch has concluded, in even starker terms:

> "[B]ased on the available evidence, the UN agency's conclusion that the ill-treatment of children who come into contact with the military detention system is 'widespread, systematic and institutionalized' appears to still be valid in 2017."

As a matter of international law it is the state of Israel and its leadership that bears the sole responsibility to ensure that its justice system for Palestinian children is compliant with international legal standards. Its ongoing track record displays a disregard for those international norms, and it is clear that the military, but most essentially the government in Israel is unwilling to consider a root and branch reform, not just of its military "justice" system, but more fundamentally, its ongoing systematic mistreatment of Palestinian children.

It is a system that lacks reform, and is unlikely to be reformed. It is a system that seeks to criminalise, and dominate. It is a brutalising system. The last word has to go to Manal Tamimi, and her view on the struggle of the Palestinian people and above all the young people involved in mass protest against the Israeli military machine:

> "That our resistance is against a system, it's against the Israeli state, it's not against the individual, so it's not against ordinary Israeli people and the time that you are standing in front of a soldier whose wearing uniform, there are Israeli activists next to you that you treat as a brother or as a friend so don't hurt the individuals, hurt the system and the uniform. It's a must for us to keep these children educated and aware and take a part within the resistance... so they will be able and capable..." [104]

Notes

1 "Hate Graffiti Sprayed in West Bank Town of Palestinian Teen: 'Death Sentence for Ahed Tamimi" – Haaretz, Sunday 11 February 2018. https://www.haaretz.com/israel-news/.premium-hate-graffiti-sprayed-in-west-bank-death-sentence-for-ahed-tamimi-1.5786555.

2 'Arab Girls who taunted helpless IDF soldiers arrested, soldiers investigated' *the Jewish Press,* 19 December 2017 – http://www.jewishpress.com/news/police-news/arab-girls-who-taunted-helpless-idf-soldiers-arrested-soldiers-investigated/2017/12/19/.

3 Bilal Tamimi you tube page – https://www.youtube.com/channel/UC9G9X7P7OVlai2E8hW5gSKA.

4 'How to be a Palestinian Supermom' HyoJin Park, Al Jazeera, 23 August 2017. http://www.aljazeera.com/indepth/features/2017/08/palestinian-supermom-170815125403131.html.

5 See for instance – Ben Ehrenreich *The Way to the Spring* – Granta 2017; Emad Burnat & Guy Davidi, *5 Broken Cameras* an Oscar nominated documentary 2011.

6 Original interview with the authors.

7 Israeli Defence Force Proclamation No. 2 – Regarding Law and Administration, 7 June 1967.

8 Virginia Tilley, Beyond Occupation – apartheid, colonialism and international law in the Occupied Palestinian Territories, Pluto Press (2012), pp. 74–78.

9 Foreign & Commonwealth Office – *Children in Military Custody* – June 2012, p. 7.

10 Original interview with Mahal Tamimi with the authors.

11 Virginia Tilley ibid p. 74.

12 Virginia Tilley ibid p. 74.

13 Art. 71 of the Fourth Geneva Convention states that "Accused persons who are prosecuted by the Occupying Power shall be promptly informed, in writing, in a language which they understand, of the particulars of the charges preferred against them."

14 See the Gate 48 report of Dutch experts – *Palestinian Children and Military Detention* (summary) April 2014. – https://www.gate48.org/wp-content/uploads/2013/06/English-RAPPORT-web.pdf.

15 See Luigi Daniele – *Enforcing Illegality: Israel's Military Justice in the West Bank* – http://www.qil-qdi.org/wp-content/uploads/2017/11/03_Israeli-Military-Justice-System_Daniele_FIN.pdf.

16 Ra'anan Alexandrowicz – *The Law in these Parts* – 2011.

17 Addameer – Political Prisoners in Israeli Prisons – June 2013.

18 Al Haq – *Waiting for Justice* – Al Haq, (Ramallah) 2005, at 258 (quoting figures from the Palestinian Ministry of Prisoners and Ex-Detainees.)

19 Virginia Tilley ibid p. 75.

20 See Fourth Geneva Convention https://www.loc.gov/rr/frd/Military_Law/pdf/GC_1949-IV.pdf.

21 See Abed Al-Rachman Al Hamed v General Security Services HCJ 1622/96 – with different criminal procedures applying in Israel and the OPT, the Israeli Supreme Court has rejected arguments that the Israeli domestic law of criminal procedure should apply to suspects arrested in the West Bank under military orders who are detained in Israel.

22 Virginia Tilley ibid p. 76.

23 Manal Tamimi interview with the authors February 2018.

24 Gaby Lasky speaking on the *Electronic Intifada* podcast 21 January 2018.

25 The Hague Conventions are the first treaties dealing with the laws of war.

26 In the judgment of *Hilu v The Government of Israel, et al.*, HCJ 302/72 and 306/72, the Israeli High Court of Justice maintained that customary international law is considered to be part of Israeli internal law without the need for any special legislation, unless contradictory to another provision in internal law.

27 Although initially Israel's voting on UN General Assembly resolutions reflected the view that the applicability of the Convention was an open question, it began from 1977 onwards to vote against its *de jure* applicability. See Adam Roberts, "Prolonged Military Occupation: The Israeli Occupied Territories 1967–1988" in Emma Playfair (ed.), *International Law and the Administration of Occupied Territory* (Clarendon Press, Oxford, 1992).

28 SC Resolution 1544 of May 2004 reiterates "the obligation of Israel, the occupying Power, to abide scrupulously by its legal obligations and responsibilities under the Fourth Geneva Convention relative to the Protection of Civilian Persons in Time of War of 12 August 1949". See also for example, GA Resolutions 56/60 of December 2001 and Resolution 58/97 of December 2003.

29 Article 4 of the Fourth Geneva Convention defines protected persons as "those civilians who, at any given moment and in any manner whatsoever find themselves, in case of a conflict or occupation, in the hands of a Party to the Conflict or Occupying Power of which they are not nationals."

30 *Legal Consequences of the Construction of a Wall in the Occupied Palestinian Territory*, ICJ Reports (2004), paragraph 95. Article 47 stipulates that protected persons in occupied territory "shall not be deprived in any case or in any manner whatsoever of the bene ts of the present Convention [...] by any agreement concluded between the authorities of the occupied territory and the Occupying Power." According to the ICRC Commentary, this provision was intended to reaffirm the

general rule expressed in Article 7 of the same Convention which states that: "no special agreement shall adversely affect the situation of protected persons [...] nor restrict the rights which it confers upon them." See Jean Pictet (ed.), *Commentary: Fourth Geneva Convention Relative to the Protection of Civilian Persons in Time of War* (ICRC, Geneva, 1958) 247.

[31] Israel ratified the International Covenant on Civil and Political Rights (ICCPR) and the International Covenant on Economic, Social and Cultural Rights (ICESCR) on 3 January 1992.

[32] Israel ratified the International Covenant on Civil and Political Rights (ICCPR) and the International Covenant on Economic, Social and Cultural Rights (ICESCR) on 3 January 1992.

[33] UNGA Official Records, 25th Session 'Respect for Human Rights in Armed Conflict: Report of the Secretary-General." UN Document A/8052, 18 September 1970, Annex 1: "General Norms Concerning Respect for Human Rights in their Applicability to Armed Conflicts." See also – General Comment 31 ICCPR Nature of the General Legal Obligation on States Parties to the Covenant – adopted 29 March 2004.

[34] When preparing its report to the UN Human Rights Committee, Israel took the position that "the Covenant and similar instruments do not apply directly to the current situation." See UN Doc. CCPR/C/SR.1675 paragraph 21. Similarly, in both its initial report to the Committee on Economic, Social and Cultural Rights in 1998 and in a further report in 2001, Israel argued that "the Palestinian population are not subject to its sovereign territory and jurisdiction" and were therefore excluded from both the report and the protection of the Covenant (UN Doc. E/C.12/1/Add.27). See also, Linda Bevis, *The Applicability of Human Rights Law to Occupied Territories: The Case of the Occupied Palestinian Territories* (Al-Haq, Ramallah, 2003). The Israeli government's position remains that neither Covenant applies in the OPT, see most recently, the transcript from the Human Rights Committee consideration of Israel's report during its Ninety-Ninth Session, 14 July 2010, at www2.ohchr.org/english/bodies/hrc/docs/CCPR.C.ISR.CO.3.doc.

[35] The Committee has expressed its view in paragraph 5 of its concluding observations on Israel's most recent report to the Committee (CCPR/C/ISR/CO/3); in paragraph 11 of its concluding observations on Israel's second periodic report (CCPR/CO/78/ISR); and in paragraph 10 of its concluding observations on Israel's initial report (CCPR/C/79/Add.93).

[36] See OCHA reports here – https://www.ochaopt.org/reports/protection-of-civilians.

[37] See Global Research – *Year-in-Review: Worst Abuses Against Palestinian Children in 2017* – 18 January 2018. https://www.globalresearch.ca/year-in-review-worst-abuses-against-palestinian-children-in-2017/5626840.

[38] The Guardian – *Palestinian girl filmed slapping Israeli soldier charged with assault* – 1 January 2018. https://www.theguardian.com/world/2018/jan/01/ahed-tamimi-palestinian-girl-filmed-slapping-israeli-soldier-is-charged-with-assault.

[39] Unicef report – *Children in Israeli Military Detention – observations and recommendations* – February 2013 p. 1.

[40] Unicef report p. 13.

[41] Military Court Watch fact sheet 2018.

[42] Foreign & Commonwealth Office – *Children in Military Custody* – June 2012 p. 9.

[43] UNCRC Art 2(1) – https://downloads.unicef.org.uk/wp-content/uploads/2010/05/UNCRC_summary.pdf.

[44] *Advisory Opinion on the Legal Consequences of Construction of a Wall in the Occupied Palestinian Territories*, dated 9 July 2004 at paragraphs 102–113.

[45] Case of Al-Skeini and other v United Kingdowm (app 55721/07) 7th July 2011 European Court of Human Rights. http://www.refworld.org/pdfid/4e2545502.pdf.

[46] Military Proclamation No. 2 Concerning Regulation of Authority and the Judiciary (West Bank) (1967) – http://nolegalfrontiers.org/military-orders/mil039ed2.html?lang=en.

[47] Military Order 1651, § 168(C).

[48] Amendments to Military Order 1651 raising the age of majority from 16 to 18 years are not specified to apply to Chapter J of Military Order 1651, which contains sentencing provisions.

[49] DCI Palestine ibid p. 12.

[50] Military Order 1651, § 212(2).

[51] Military Order 1651, § 212(3).

[52] Military Order 1651, § 215(D).

[53] Article 76 of the Fourth Geneva Convention states: "Protected persons accused of offences shall be detained in the occupied country, and if convicted shall serve their sentences therein." Pursuant to Article 147 of the Fourth Geneva Convention, unlawfully transferring a protected person is a grave breach of the Convention and attracts personal criminal responsibility. Under Article 146, all parties to the Convention have a positive legal obligation to search out and prosecute those responsible for grave breaches.

[54] DCI Palestine – No way to treat a Child – p. 16.

[55] Interview with the authors in Nabi Saleh.

[56] DCI Palestine – No way to Treat a Child – p20. https://d3n8a8pro7vhmx.cloudfront.net/dcipalestine/pages/1527/attachments/original/1460665378/DCIP_NWTTAC_Report_Final_April_2016.pdf?1460665378.

[57] CRC – articles 19 and 37(a).

58 Committee on the Rights of the Child no.10, para. 89. http://www.refworld.org/docid/4670fca12.html.

59 UNICEF, *Children in Military Detention Observations and Recommendations Bulletin No. 2: February 2015*, at 1 (2015), https://www.unicef.org/oPt/UNICEF_oPt_Children_in_Israeli_Military_Detention_Observations_and_Recommendations_-_6_March_2013.pdf.

60 The UNICEF Bulletin no.2 – p.2. Update at: https://www.unicef.org/oPt/Children_in_Israeli_Military_Detention_-_Observations_and_Recommendations_-_Bulletin_No._2_-_February_2015.pdf.

61 UNICEF Bulletin no2 – p. 7.

62 See DCI Palestine *ibid* and Unicef *ibid*.

63 http://www.militarycourtwatch.org/page.php?id=MmNuAkpGrsa613395AWw2bO0pT3K data collected by the West Bank-based organisation Military Court Watch ("MCW") has monitored issues of concern based on 530 child testimonies collected between 2013–2017.

64 DCI Palestine *ibid* p. 21.

65 DCI Palestine *ibid* pp. 3-15 – show a series of amendments to Military Order 1651 in order to allay complaints of the international community, these include, establishing a juvenile court – order 1644; raising the age of majority – order 1676; a maximum detention period (order 1726) and Audio-video recording f interrogations (order 1745) the claim is nothing on the ground has fundamentally changed.

66 DCI Palestine *ibid* p. 21.

67 Convention against Torture and other Cruel, Inhuman or Degrading Treatment or Punishment. (see Part I, Article 1 for instance) http://www.ohchr.org/EN/ProfessionalInterest/Pages/CAT.aspx.

68 DCI (2013) reported that this was the case in no less than 97.2% of the 108 cases studied by them. In a previous sample of DCI (2012), tie-raps were used to bind the hands of arrested children in 95% of the 311 studied cases. See also: UNICEF 2013, p. 10 and B'Tselem 2011, p. 27.

69 DCI Palestine No Way to Treat a Child – p24. See also UNICEF 2013; UN Committee on the Rights of the Child 2013, par. 35, 36 and 73.

70 Foreign & Commonwealth Office ind para 48 p. 14.

71 UN Committee on the Rights of the Child 2013, par. 35, 36 and 73, at the start and under d.

72 The Times of Israel – *6-year-old Boy arrested, held for 8 hours* – 30 April 2015.

73 Jaclynn Ashly – Palestinian Ahed Tamimi arrested by Israeli forces – 20 December 2017 – Al Jazeera news – http://www.aljazeera.com/news/2017/12/palestinian-ahed-tamimi-arrested-israeli-forces-171219174834758.html.

[74] DCI Palestine *Palestinian children detained in the Israeli military court system*, 25 June 2013 reported, on the basis of 108 statements, that during arrest, transport or interrogation in 74.1% physical force was used and in 67.6% verbal force was used by soldiers.

[75] See Military Court Watch statistics here http://www.militarycourtwatch.org/page.php?id=MmNuAkpGrsa613395AWw2bO0pT3K.

[76] B'tselem & HaMoked – report *Unprotected: The Detention of Palestinian Teenagers in East Jerusalem.*
https://www.btselem.org/download/201710_unprotected_summary_eng.pdf

[77] DCI Palestine *ibid* p. 25.

[78] Convention on the Rights of the Child, see Art. 3- http://www.ohchr.org/EN/ProfessionalInterest/Pages/CRC.aspx.

[79] Linah Alsaafin – Palestinian minors arrested by Israel suffer abuse – 25 October 2017. http://www.aljazeera.com/news/2017/10/palestinian-minors-arrested-israel-suffer-abuse-171024215105404.html.

[80] Breaking the silence – *Children and Youth Soldiers' Testimonies 2005-2011* http://www.breakingthesilence.org.il/wp-content/uploads/2012/08/Children_and_Youth_Soldiers_Testimonies_2005_2011_Eng.pdf.

[81] Military Court Watch *ibid.*

[82] Lawyers for Palestinian Human Rights – *Israel's military detention of Palestinian children living in the occupied Palestinian territory* – pt 23. https://lphr.org.uk/wp-content/uploads/2018/02/LPHR-full-briefing-on-Israels-military-detention-of-Palestinian-children-living-in-the-occupied-Palestinian-territory-Feb-2018.pdf.

[83] No Legal Frontiers – *All Guilty! Observations in the Military Juvenile Court 2010/11* – July 2011, to be consulted at: http://nolegalfrontiers.org/reports/77-report-juvenile-court9ed2.html?lang=en – According to this report, in 65 of the 70 studied cases, witness statements (often of other arrested children) were used as evidence.

[84] Foreign & Commonwealth Office – *Children in Military Custody* – June 2012 p. 17.

[85] Manal Tamimi – interview with the authors – February 2018.

[86] Manal Tamimi – interview with the authors.

[87] DCI Palestine p. 40 (2016). During interrogation, in 96 out of 429 cases (22.4 percent), interrogators threatened children, and in 123 out of 429 cases (28.7 percent) children were subjected to verbal abuse or intimidation.

[88] DCI Palestine p. 40 (2016).

[89] DCI Palestine p. 46 (2016) In 144 out of 429 cases (33.6 percent), children were shown or forced to sign documentation written in Hebrew. Interrogations are typically conducted in Arabic, but sometimes in Hebrew with an Arabic translator since the vast majority of Palestinian children do not speak Hebrew. During the interrogation, an interrogator often prepares the children's statements in Hebrew with no verbal or written translation provided to the child. These documents often contain incriminating statements or confessions.

[90] DCI Palestine p. 36 (2016).

[91] Convention on the Rights of the Child, art. 37(c).

[92] Military Order 1651, §§ 58(C)-(D) & 59 (C)-(D).

[93] DCI Palestine ibid (2016) pp. 46-47.

[94] *See* Convention on the Rights of the Child; Committee on the Rights of the Child, *General Comment No. 10*, U.N. Doc. CRC/C/GC/10 (Apr. 25, 2007), http://www2. ohchr.org/english/bodies/crc/docs/CRC.C.GC.10.pdf.

[95] Committee on the Rights of the Child, *General Comment No. 10*, ¶ 83, U.N. Doc. CRC/C/GC/10 (Apr. 25, 2007), http://www2. ohchr.org/english/bodies/crc/docs/ CRC.C.GC.10.pdf.

[96] DCI Palestine *ibid* (2016) pp. 47-48.

[97] DCI Palestine *ibid* (2016) pp. 47-48.

[98] see testimonies of soldiers – Breaking the silence – *Children and Youth Soldiers' Testimonies 2005–2011.*

[99] DCI Palestine *ibid* (2016) p. 49.

[100] DCI Palestine *ibid* (2016) p. 49.

[101] DCI Palestine *ibid* (2016) p. 50.

[102] Military Order 1651, § 212(2) & (3).

[103] UK Parliamentary report ibid (2013).

[104] Manal Tamimi interview with the authors.

CHAPTER 4

Women and the Struggle to Liberate Palestine

What has it felt like for Ahed to be arrested? What has her experience been like in military prison system? Ahed's aunt, Manal Tamimi has first-hand experience. In fact, she has been arrested three times. Here she tells us some detail from her most recent experience of arrest and prison.

Moreover, Manal widens the scope of her account to consider the situation of women like her in the struggle for an end to the Occupation and the liberation of Palestine.

This chapter, from Manal, gives a wider emancipatory perspective to the struggles of young women like Ahed. Ahed, is a public focal point of a generation of girls and young women who, whilst willing to protest or resist alongside men against the occupation, will no longer accept playing a subservient, or secondary role. Ahed is one of many, who fight back.

When I was arrested, in December 2017, for the third time, I was at a protest outside the military court at Ofer prison, Jerusalem. The soldiers had shot tear gas and I wanted to move away. They wanted me to stay put, but this would have meant me having to breathe in the gas. They arrested me, I thought that it was because I disobeyed their order. But when they began to interrogate me I found out that the soldiers had been filming me on their mobiles, directly, filming my face. Actually, they were following me, and they knew exactly who I was. When we were away from cameras, the soldiers began to hit me and beat me up which caused bleeding in my jaw and it was swollen. I had to go to the prison clinic twice, they gave me the wrong medicine which caused bleeding in my stomach. I was held for just one week, but it was the one of the most difficult experiences, because I was exhausted, all the time.

When they take you to the court, it's another form of punishment. It was 2.30am, the middle of the night, and they took us in a metal bus, without windows. We were handcuffed all the time, and they adjusted the air conditioning so it was very cold. It was raining and you are in a metal cage, in a freezing, metal, military bus. They transported us from one prison, then to another. Finally, we are left in in a very cold cell, its floor – full of water, so all the time you're sitting with wet legs. They kept us until 7 or 8pm, into the start of the night, in that cold, wet cell. Then we returned back, the very same way, and arrived, where we started, at 11.30pm or midnight. So, after almost 24 hours of this transportation I was very tired – exhausted. It's emotionally draining, because you can't sleep, they give us one meal, which is just to keep us alive – so it's very, very difficult.

It's difficult, but I am strong. I am a woman, and we are stronger than men, we can handle the pain of giving birth. Also, how we work shows our strength. Most women handle different jobs at one time and they're taking care of their families, taking care of their children. By the end she's the one who is raising the new generation and, if she is capable of raising children and teaching them, with a new vision, and a new personality – she can handle any other kind of leadership, leadership of uprisings.

Palestinian history has known two major popular uprisings, during which we tried to liberate our land and our country. There have been two mass uprisings in the occupied territory. The first Intifada started in 1987 and, as BBC news reflected in a later news story:

> "The Palestinians were largely unarmed, so the enduring picture of the Intifada is one of young men and boys throwing stones and rocks at Israeli troops." [1]

This of course is not completely true. In the first Intifada women played a leading role too, as I hope to explain. I will also explain how women are still playing a leading role in harnessing the strength of the Palestinian people in the villages and in the refugee camps.

The first Intifada continued until approximately 1993, and dissipated with the proposed potential of the Oslo Accords.

The role of Palestinian women evolved in the context of the development and expansion of popular participation in all areas of the West Bank and Gaza Strip, leading to the formation of the – *Women's Supreme Council for Women's Frameworks in the Palestinian Liberation Organisation (PLO)*.

During this period, Palestinian women's organisations began to develop with the help of non-governmental organisations (NGOs). These organisations were organised around issues of research into the struggle, training, developing organisational skills and awareness-raising. These groups contributed positively to the graduation of many leading activists, who at that stage were largely linked to a certain commitment to parties and organisations in the national movement.

The second Intifada began in September 2000 following the provocative visit by Ariel Sharon to the Temple Mount, in close vicinity with the Al-Aqsa mosque. The second Intifada concluded in 2005.

For women, the experience of the second Intifada was not as clear, as their role was not in the leadership positions. In many ways the second Intifada was far more militarised, and the occupation forces concentrated on a clear military escalation. This response contributed to the destruction of the Palestinian territories, both in terms of human life and the infrastructure. There was re-occupation of the Palestinian cities and communities that were evacuated under the Oslo Agreement.

It seems that the Palestinian struggle was not best served in the second Intifada by it being a largely military campaign. The Palestinian leadership was unable to balance the military action of the resistance, on the one hand, and the political action of the resistance and negotiator on the other, to reach political results on the ground. The women's role was limited because it was militarised and not all women were able to participate. Some women took a part in this Intifada but many women couldn't take a part especially when it became so militarised. For the first one or two months it was similar to the First Intifada for women but after that it tended to be militarised and women couldn't take part fully.

In my view the role of Palestinian women in the second Intifada, was less, and there were many restrictions on it, contrary to their prominent participation in the first Intifada. This was due to the emergence of Islamic movements, some of which refused women's participation. In spite of this, the second Intifada witnessed the participation of women even amongst women who supported *Hamas*. Indeed, 460 women were killed during the second Intifada, and the number of cases of detention included almost. This reflects that despite women not playing a leading role, because of the nature of the Intifada, they still sacrificed a great deal. This was acknowledged throughout Palestinian society.

As a general view, the first and second Intifada came as a result of the continued occupation of Palestine. It also reflected the deterioration of the situation in the country. In both of these movements the Palestinian people rose up against injustice, occupation, oppression, murder, administrative detention, unemployment and difficult living conditions.

The history of the uprisings witnessed many fluctuations in the experience of women and their participation. Certainly, many women joined the military resistance. However, there was the beginning of a change in the strategy of the Palestinian people as how best to fight back.

That new strategy, in my view, took its inspiration from the first Intifada which was characterised with women being on the frontline in the resistance, as well as playing key roles strategically, along with the traditional social roles. Throughout the first Intifada the role of women increasingly became central. However, in the second Intifada, women were restricted, and in my view, they were not in the frontline of the resistance as much as they should have been.

Today, Palestine is witnessing a great popular uprising, but on a localised basis. Also, we have the asset of the tremendous development in technology. We can now film, edit, tweet and post our struggle immediately in the internet. We can also show the world how brutal the Israeli armed forces are.

The October 2015 uprising saw the return of Palestinian women to the top of participation in the national struggle, and standing side by side with men in the face of the Israeli occupation and for the liberation of Palestine. The social media and the social networking sites were able to transmit images of young women and girls in the frontline of protest against the Israeli occupation forces. They faced down the soldiers without fear, they threw stones when faced with tear gas, and even at times paid the ultimate price, with their lives. Perhaps one of the most famous Palestinian women who turned into a symbol and role model in this uprising is Dalia Nassar,[2] who was wounded by Israeli soldiers with a bullet to the chest.

The uprising continues in the Palestinian territories, and the Palestinian women continue to fight on the frontline in order to defend our towns and villages, and to seek the independence of Palestine.

The heroic role played by Palestinian women in the uprising was not of course the beginning of their march in the history of the Palestinian people and its revolution. It is since the very beginning of the occupation of Palestine that women have, and have continued, to play an important role alongside the men in every location and time. Palestinian women play a leading role in the struggle through all forms of local and national action. They struggle also, as mothers, to raise their children to the challenge. We are involved in the student and women's organisations. But crucially, women are on the *frontline* of the national masses in occupied Palestine.

Palestinian women activists were able to form and create women's organisations in all locations, and this led to the formation of the Palestinian Women's Union in the camps, the villages and the cities. The Women's Union for Social Action has also emerged and participated through its contribution to the strategy of mass non-violent action across Palestine, against the occupation. In addition to that role the Women's Union have also been at the forefront of establishing kindergartens in many cities, villages and camps – to ensure that women can play a role in the struggle.

I would also say that the women of Palestine have provided the necessary conditions and strategy for providing education not just for our next generation, but also internationally, in order to combat any ignorance or misunderstanding as to what this occupation is all about.

It is important to know that for the struggle against occupation to succeed, that we are united. But to be united it is important that we combat any restriction on the role of women in the resistance. We must combat and address all the negative inherited factors of social oppression. But in any reform process we have to acknowledge that does not solve the basic issues of women's freedom, nor does it achieve equality in civil and social rights. The liberation of women must also be linked first and foremost to addressing the crisis of our society in all its dimensions. We cannot talk about the liberation of women if it is in isolation from the occupation, but in order to liberate Palestine from occupation, women must continue to play a leading role.

The real liberation of women, therefore, is freedom from social oppression. We need equal rights with men, decision-making in all fields and at all levels, and participation in political, economic, cultural, social and family activities. This is the expression of the issues that Palestinian women face, but it is linked closely to the wider issue for our national independence, social progress, development, social justice and democracy. Equally, our national liberation must solve the wider problems of poverty, the poor distribution of wealth, and lack of social justice. However, the role of women and their treatment cannot be separated from the dialectical interdependence between politics, the economy, national liberation on the one hand, and ensuring internal societal democracy on the other hand.

In addition, the activities of poor Palestinian women in the camps and villages of the West Bank and Gaza played a prominent and tangible role on a daily basis in resisting the occupation throughout the period of the first Intifada. Their role was often characterised by spontaneous organisation, both through informal forms and through NGOs or other women's groups.

Despite the actions and activities of many Palestinian women, women's participation in the second Intifada was less, and more restricted, than their participation in the first Intifada. This can partly be explained by the growth of some Islamic movements which began to appear strongly during this period. As a result, the adoption by some of political Islam placed restrictions on the participation of women in the uprising.

Palestinian women have formed many associations and institutions to help the families of those who have been killed during the first and second uprisings. We aim to ensure their children, and families are cared for. That they are not left isolated.

There is no doubt that the living reality of Palestinian women is difficult in all parts of their lives. However, that experience varies from are to area. Women, on a daily basis, are subjected to very great challenges – but there is no doubt that the liberation of Palestine cannot be achieved without women being central to the resistance to occupation.

The current resistance to the occupation is localized; from village, to town, to refugee camp. In my view the women have played a leading role within the resistance since the beginning. If you follow the Palestinian resistance history from the British mandate, through the Intifadas, particularly the first one, and most recently with mass peaceful resistance you will find that women are the backbone of the movement. When mass non-violent resistance became the next stage of the resistance the women's role began to take its part.

Here in the village (Nabi Saleh) women have played a leading role, since the beginning it was very important that they took part in all the activities because we are a small community and the whole village is one family, so this makes us united, and a very strong community. We are united, we are used to doing everything together, so that when we took the decision to begin the non-violent resistance there was no discussion as to whether or not women should take part – it was obvious. It was not whether women should be involved, it was about what is the strategy? The theme and what we should do? That's why the women took a very important role and most of the time we were in the front line. I was in the frontline in the protest along with other women from the village.

However, when I am on the protests in Nabi Saleh I also feel safe because everybody surrounding me will be someone close to me, there will be my husband, my brother, my son, my uncle, my cousin. I am scared for them but, at the same time I know the minute something bad happens to me or to one of us, we will all immediately help. However as a woman we face the same thing the men face by being arrested, by being shot at or even killed. We are equal to the men, but if a husband is arrested or injured the woman becomes the man of the family, she supports the family if he's injured and also she needs to be very strong to handle the situation. Once an American Congressman said to me, that the woman, she is the neck and the man is the head, it does not matter how big the brain is if the neck is broken, the whole body dies. This is the same situation in this struggle.

The entry of girls and young women into the liberation struggle is very important. The new generation did not grow up with the Oslo Accords. The entry into the struggle of our daughters means the liberation stage begins from the day they are born – they are not weighed down by the past. All of them endure the intensity of the occupation and its siege, however we must ensure that more young people are involved in defeating it.

The United Nations Special Rapporteur on adequate housing has repeatedly stressed the impact of house demolitions on women, children and the elderly, and the consequent increase in the economic and psychological burden on Palestinian women. According to a statistical report issued by the Israeli Committee for House demolitions 351 structures have been demolished, 528 people displaced, and since 1967 over 48,000 homes have been demolished.[3]

Due to poverty and difficult living conditions, families who have lost their homes are forced to move to live with relatives, who often do not have enough space to accommodate another family; which causes discomfort and psychological distress for these families. According to the Palestinian Central Bureau of Statistics (PCBS), while 454,697 families will need to build new housing units over the next ten years, only 117,909 families will be able to do so.

It is known that the Palestinian family depends on agriculture as a source of basic livelihood; women play a prominent role in this sector. They stand alongside their husband in the cultivation and service of the land and in the care and supervision of cattle. This is why the policy of confiscating land and bulldozing by the occupation authorities, the source of her family's livelihood, causes a great economic and psychological crisis.

Despite the Israeli government's claim that the Wall will not affect land ownership or the residents' access to their livelihoods, it has confiscated more than 230 km of the most fertile land in the West Bank (about 15% of all West Bank agricultural land).

The Wall also made it impossible for Palestinians in its proximity to access 95% of their water resources for irrigated agriculture. As a result, more than 7,000 Palestinian families lost their livelihoods. A report by the International Labor Office pointed to the particular harm to women as a result; as women constitute the majority of the labor force in agriculture.

The United Nations Secretary-General's 2006 report on assistance to the Palestinian people stated that the continued closure of land in the Gaza Strip and the West Bank and the prevention of movement between them paralyzed the ability of the Palestinian health system to operate at the required level.

According to the Palestinian Central Bureau of Statistics (PCBS) and the International Labor Organization (ILO), restrictions on freedom of movement through checkpoints/closures have been a major obstacle to Palestinian access to health services. 52.5% of households report closures, 53.6% of households in the West Bank close to the Wall. Obstacles to access to health and rural services, especially for women in isolated villages hit hard, especially with checkpoints on the cities in which hospitals are located. These restrictions lead to delayed access to urgent cases by medical staff and ambulance personnel. This results in ambulances being forced to conduct long detours; and transporting patients from one ambulance to another.

Two people from my own village have died as a result of road blocks and check points preventing speedy transport to hospital. Mariam Tamimi, a 59-year-old mother and grandmother, suffered a heart attack and was stopped for an hour at a road block and passed away before getting to hospital. Hussein Tamimi, a 50-year-old teacher, also a father, suffered a heart attack but was forced on a long way round to hospital due to obstacles and checkpoints. His journey was interrupted with questioning at check points, and he died on a journey that had already taken three hours. The journey from Nabi Saleh to Ramallah, where the hospital is, ought to be 30 minutes.

Pregnant Palestinian women, especially at the late stage of their pregnancy, are affected by this policy. Many pregnant women have been forced to deliver their babies at checkpoints in an environment that lacks the minimum hygiene, medical and medical care required of the mother and the newborn.

The report on the issue of pregnant Palestinian women giving birth at Israeli checkpoints, issued by the United Nations High Commissioner for Human Rights on 23 February 2007, noted that between 2000 and 2006, 69 pregnant Palestinian women delivered at checkpoints. According to data from the Health Information Center of the Palestinian Ministry of Health, 35 babies have died at checkpoints. Mothers did not receive the urgent care needed for their condition; five women died at birth; and six pregnant women were injured at checkpoints; they were beaten, shot and even poisoned by Israeli soldiers.

Approximately 10% of pregnant women wanting to give birth in the hospital have to wait for two to four hours before access to health facilities; about 6% of pregnant women need more than four hours to reach those facilities; while before the Al-Aqsa (second) Intifada, the average time required for access to health facilities was between 15 and 30 minutes. Fear of such problems has led to a preference, for a large number of pregnant Palestinian women, to deliver at home. Women living in villages, rural areas and villages in the West Bank, besieged by the apartheid wall, suffer enormously from this problem. The journey takes many hours and becomes *impossible* at night.

Acknowledging the suffering of Palestinian women under occupation, the United Nations on the situation of women (45 members) adopted a draft resolution entitled "Situation of and assistance to Palestinian women". The outcome of the voting at the conclusion of its fifty-seventh session, held at United Nations Headquarters in New York from 4 March to 15 March 2013, was as follows: 25 in favor of resolution 2, against – the United States of America, Abstention – Japan, Finland, Republic of Korea, Spain, Estonia, Germany, Italy, Belgium, Netherlands, Georgia. The resolution reaffirms that the Israeli occupation continues to be the main obstacle to the transformation, advancement and self-reliance of Palestinian women and their participation in the development of their society.

In our time, social media, like what happened in the so-called Arab Spring, has become the first platform for everything that happens in Palestine. Therefore, if this gift achieves the conditions of the Intifada, we are about to witness a real uprising supported by an electronic uprising.

After trying to impose restrictions on Palestinian women and restrict their role in social activities by Israeli authorities, today's girls in Palestine are taking to the streets to free themselves from these restrictions. The liberation of Palestine includes a process of freedom from injustice on all sectors of the population, including women. Confrontations are proof that those who promote the idea that women are not qualified to participate in the fight against the enemy. Any people, Arab men included, who believe that excluding women from the liberation process, that it is exclusively an honor for men – they will have to rethink their calculations well.

In the past, and present weeks, we have seen pictures of girls leading the confrontations of the Palestinian people against the occupation authorities, published by activists on their pages on Facebook and Twitter. We also saw the shameful comments by a good number of Arab youth who were provoked by the dress of these girls and their hair at the time, when these girls went out because the enemy provoked their patriotism and religion. The young girls and women, proved by their participation in struggle, that a symbol for less reason, and religion, in the current equation is the man sitting in front of his screen. The women tell themselves what they should do, not anyone else.

The women of Palestine today, as they did in the last decades, did not and will not ask for your opinion and your consent to participate in the protection of their country. They will stand up in jeans and robes. They will stand up with the *kaffiyeh* and the *hijab*. They will stand up against injustice and fight for freedom.

But I will leave the final words to Ahed:

> "Right now, injustice is happening all across the world. We should extend our struggles to one another in order to end all of the world's injustices. We are all victims of some kind of occupation. We won't let anyone suffer alone." [4]

Notes

[1] BBC news 6th May 2008. – http://news.bbc.co.uk/1/hi/world/middle_east/7381369.stm.

[2] https://www.alaraby.co.uk/english/blog/2015/10/21/palestinian-shot-in-heart-vows-to-continue-resistance.

[3] See https://icahd.org.

[4] Interview with FOSNA, 2016.

QR Codes to videos

QR code 1
The website for the book with extra material
http://www.ahedtamimibook.com/

QR Code 2
Petition to Free Ahed and all the children in Israeli jails
https://secure.avaaz.org/campaign/en/free_ahed/?fzUBPab

QR Code 3
Ahed Tamimi - Living Resistance Tour
https://www.youtube.com/watch?v=cMWuk_mi5kw

QR Code 4
TeleSUR English: Ahed Tamimi
https://www.youtube.com/watch?v=yV1HwG1_phs

QR Code 5
11-year-old Ahed Tamimi: Where is my brother?
https://www.youtube.com/watch?v=E4FM9WGRWdQ

QR Code 6
11-year-old Ahed tries to prevent soldiers from arresting her mother
https://www.youtube.com/watch?v=Bh9pwEPpn0Q

QR Code 7
Ahed helps to free her little brother
https://www.youtube.com/watch?v=YG4sQkoWAU4

QR Code 8
15 and 19 December 2017: Ahed confronting Israeli soldiers and
getting arrested
https://www.youtube.com/watch?v=8YM41wofiXw

QR Code 9
FRANCE 24 English: Ahed Tamimi's arrest
https://www.youtube.com/watch?v=OPTC4nJzFWY&t=14s

QR Code 10
Ahed Tamimi Trial: Court orders teenager to remain in custody
https://www.youtube.com/watch?v=0CxHYTI_LnE

QR Code 11
TRT World: What happened to Ahed Tamimi after her arrest?
https://www.youtube.com/watch?v=MxhNRs-j6b4

QR Code 12
Palestinian prisoner of conscience Bassem Tamimi speaks out
https://www.youtube.com/watch?v=cvOMdTRwLwo

QR Code 13
Nariman Tamimi Interview
https://www.youtube.com/watch?v=v-VpIlz5zyA

QR Code 14
Prevented from reaching the water spring
https://www.youtube.com/watch?v=BxVtoG0aGsg

QR Code 15
Prevented from reaching the water spring 2
https://www.youtube.com/watch?v=4r7oFaX2t1c

QR Code 16
South African TV: Interview with Palestinian Resistance icon Ahed
Tamimi
https://www.youtube.com/watch?v=5NtCcRaZ7MI

Ahed Tamimi challenging an Israeli Defence Force (IDF) soldier of the occupation. (Photo: Haim Schwarczenberg.)

Ahed demands that IDF soldiers leave her property, 15 December 2017. A still from the video which went viral. (Photo: Nariman Tamimi.)

Ahed appears at Ofer military court, Jerusalem. 1 January 2018.
(Photo: Ahmad Gharabi.)

15-year-old Mohamed Tamimi, with his mother, after release from hospital following life saving surgery. He had been shot in the face by an IDF soldier. January 2018. (Photo: Heidi Levine.)

Ahed struggles to prevent the arrest of her mother Nariman.

Ahed on a speaking tour of South Africa, Accord House, Durban. 2017.

UK Labour Party Members of Parliament express solidarity with the Tamimi family, following Ahed's arrest. This message/photograph is on the living room table in Ahed's family home.

Ahed's father Bassem Tamimi with authors, Paul Morris and Paul Heron.
The placard shows the number who had signed the petition demanding Ahed's
release. February 2018.

The observation balloon over the Israeli settlement of Halamish keeping a watch on the Palestinian village of Nabi Saleh. February 2018. (Photo: Paul Morris.)

Entrance to Halamish settlement, photographed from car on the way to Nabi Saleh. February 2018. (Photo: Paul Heron.)

IDF military watchtower at entrance to Nabi Saleh. February 2018.
(Photo: Paul Heron.)

Graffiti death threats aimed at Ahed, written in Hebrew – spray painted over by Nabi
Saleh villagers. February 2018. (Photo: Paul Heron.)

Author, Manal Tamimi with her husband, Bilal Tamimi. Bilal is well known for his filming and recording of the protests in Nabi Saleh which can be seen on his YouTube page (Tamimi 1966). February 2018. (Photo: Paul Heron.)

Mohammad Tamimi, aged 19, (one of Manal and Bilal's sons) defiant as IDF soldiers arrest him in the night from the family home. January 2018. (Photo: Manal Tamimi.)

Poster demanding the release of
Mohammad Tamimi. February 2018.

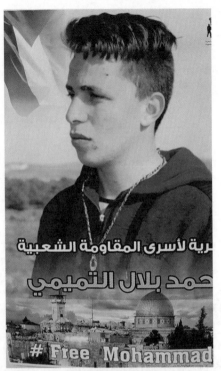

ــرية لأسرى المقاومة الشعبية

ـحمد بلال التميمي

Free Mohammad

Osama (22) and Mohammad Tamimi (19), brothers, on the hillside of Nabi Saleh.
Currently detained in Israeli military jails. (Photo: Bilal Tamimi.)

Janna Jihad Ayyad, aged 11 (referred to by Vice News as the youngest journalist in Palestine) with mother Nawal in Nabi Saleh. February 2018. (Photo: Paul Morris.)

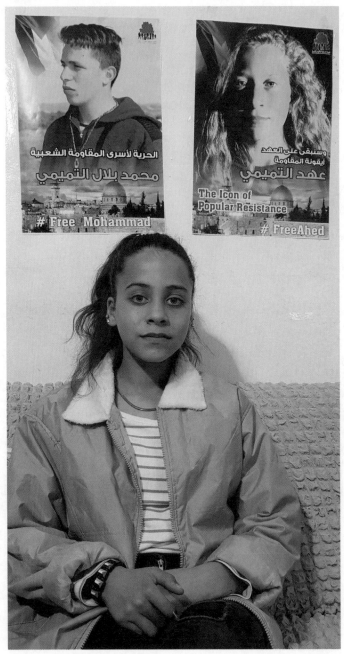

Janna with posters demanding the release of Ahed and Mohammad Tamimi. February 2018. (Photo: Paul Morris.)

Some of the many tear gas canisters collected by the youth of Nabi Saleh and displayed as a symbol of resistance. February 2018. (Photo: Paul Morris.)

Tear gas canisters in the hallway of Manal and Bilal's home. February 2018. (Photo: Paul Morris.)

Metal bars and a mesh placed across the window to prevent tear gas entering a family home in Nabi Saleh. February 2018. (Photo: Paul Morris.)

Boys taking a break from an evening football game in the street at Nabi Saleh – from left to right, Mohammad (12), Kenan (11), Mohammad (11), Salem (11). February 2018. (Photo: Paul Heron.)

Protest posters demanding the release of Ahed and over 300 other Palestinian children held in military prison by the occupying Israeli forces. This protest poster replaced the official advertisements at London bus stops. January 2018 (Photo: @protestencil.)

London double-decker waits at bus stop which demands *Free Ahed*. February 2018. (Photo: @protestencil.)

International protests demand *Free Ahed Tamimi! Palestine Will Overcome!* Lisbon, Portugal. March 2018. (Photo: Ruth Woolhouse.)